Psychoanalytic Perspectives on Women

CURRENT ISSUES IN PSYCHOANALYTIC PRACTICE
Monographs of the Society for Psychoanalytic Training

1. CURRENT AND HISTORICAL PERSPECTIVES ON THE BORDERLINE PATIENT, *edited by Reuben Fine, Ph.D.*
2. PSYCHOANALYTIC APPROACHES TO SUPERVISION *edited by Robert C. Lane, Ph.D.*
3. PSYCHOANALYTIC APPROACHES TO ADDICTION *edited by Angelo Smaldino, Ph.D.*

CURRENT ISSUES IN PSYCHOANALYTIC PRACTICE

Monographs of the Society for Psychoanalytic Training
Number 4

Psychoanalytic Perspectives on Women

Edited by
Elaine V. Siegel, Ph.D.

BRUNNER/MAZEL, PUBLISHERS • NEW YORK

Library of Congress Cataloging-in-Publication Data
Psychoanalytic perspectives on women / edited by Elaine V. Siegel.
p. cm. — (Current issues in psychoanalytic practice ; no. 4)
Includes bibliographical references.
ISBN 0-87630-655-5
1. Women and psychoanalysis. 2. Women—Sexual behavior.
I. Siegel, Elaine V. II. Series: Current issues in psychoanalytic practice (Brunner/Mazel Publishers) ; no. 4
[DNLM: 1. Psychoanalytic Interpretation. 2. Psychoanalytic Therapy—case studies. 3. Women—psychology. W1 CU788LD no. 4 / WM 460.5.W6 P9732]
RC451.4.W6P765 1992
616.89'17'082—dc20
DNLM/DLC
for Library of Congress 91-43418
CIP

Published by
BRUNNER/MAZEL, INC.
19 Union Square
New York, NY 10003

Manufactured in the United States of America

10 9 8 7 6 5 4 3 2 1

This book is dedicated to the
indomitable spirit in women everywhere.

DAUGHTERS

It was an odd dusk
Diffuse skylight hung between grey
  wadded clouds
And sprayed a fractious calm across the sea

The smell of gardenias drew me out
White, sticky, suffocating
I couldn't work I couldn't think
I remembered lovers walking hand in hand
And sperm trickling down my thigh
I pictured the house where I lived alone
Through need not choice

It was then I saw
The terrible heart within my mother's soul
That tried me and bound me
Before it was my privilege to see

The fault was in the wound
In the smell of the gardenias
And in the rain that pelted down my eyelids.

A poem by Melanie
who was wise beyond her years

Contents

Contributors

Penny W. Caccavo, M.S.W. Faculty member and supervisor, The New York Center for Psychoanalytic Training; member and former director of the Society for Psychoanalytic Training's Liberal Arts and Sciences Program; fellow, New York Society of Clinical Social Work Psychotherapists; member, Division 39 of the American Psychological Association; former school psychologist; staff member, Ecumenical Consultation Center; psychoanalyst in private practice.

Carolyn Celentano, A.C.S.W. Faculty member, The New York Center for Psychoanalytic Training; social worker and psychoanalyst who practices, teaches, and resides in Suffolk County on Long Island, New York.

Theodore L. Dorpat, M.D. Training and supervising analyst and a former director of the Seattle Institute for Psychoanalysis; Clinical Professor of Psychiatry at the University of Washington; and in private practice of psychoanalysis, psychiatry, and forensic psychiatry. He is the author or co-author of over 200 scientific publications.

Laura Arens Fuerstein, M.S.W. Training and control analyst and faculty member of The New York Center for Psychoanalytic Training and The Institute for Psychoanalysis and Psychotherapy of New Jersey; instructor, Hunter College Post-Masters Advanced Clinical Social Work Program; member, Division 39 of the American Psychological Association; senior member of The Society for Psychoanalytic Training; and in private practice in New York City and Highland Park, New Jersey. She is the author of numerous professional papers, including those on gender differences and eroticism in the therapeutic relationship.

Florence Holland Former director of New York City's Department of Correction's House of Detention for Women. She trained as a psychoanalytic psychotherapist at the Institute for the Study of Psychotherapy and maintained an active private practice. She also published prose and poetry until her death in 1979.

Susan Kavaler-Adler, Ph.D. Founding director, Object Relations Institute for Psychoanalysis and Psychotherapy; faculty member and supervisor for the National Institute for the Psychotherapies (NIP); faculty of the Psychoanalytic Institute of the Postgraduate Center for Mental Health; member of the board of directors, supervisor, and faculty for the Brooklyn Institute of Psychotherapy and Psychoanalysis; private practice of psychotherapy, psychoanalysis, and writers groups and object relations seminars; on board of Women and Psychoanalysis, Division 39 of the American Psychological Association.

Kenneth R. King, M.D. Training and supervising analyst and Chairman, Division of Child and Adolescent Analysis, Seattle Institute for Psychoanalysis; associate clinical faculty of the University of Washington; and in private practice in child, adolescent, and adult psychoanalysis. His special interests include early child development, the impact of trauma upon development, and the application of contemporary object relations theory to clinical technique.

Ronald W. Levin, M.D. Faculty of the Seattle Institute for Psychoanalysis and Clinical Assistant Professor of Psychiatry and Behavioral Sciences at the University of Washington. He is trained in both internal medicine and psychiatry and has an interest in psychosomatic and addictive pathology.

Sidney M. Rosenblatt, Ph.D. Director of Mental Health Service, Lavelle School for the Blind; senior member and faculty member of The Society for Psychoanalytic Training; and in private practice.

Elaine V. Siegel, Ph.D. Senior analyst and former board member at The New York Center for Psychoanalytic Training. She has published widely and lectures on human development and psychoanalysis both here and abroad.

Introduction

Elaine V. Siegel, Ph.D.

Guest Editor

It is my pleasure to introduce a collection of case studies and essays dealing with the inner life of women. Included are five outstanding reports of women whose psychological journey toward mature femaleness was hampered, almost destroyed, by developmental and other traumas. Two essays speak of the many symbolisms by which we in this society understand the evolution of a girl child into a woman. A third essay brilliantly speaks of the psychologic travail and possible developmental lag of some women artists.

The contributions have in common new psychoanalytic views of how a woman develops. However, Freud was the first to investigate the inner world of women and, as McDougall (1986) has made us aware, was indebted to them for his insights leading to the concept of the unconscious. But he appears to have felt somewhat intimidated by his subject. His metaphors for the female genital, for instance, represent a void, a dark continent, a lack. Yet he was dissatisfied with regard to his theories about women. He was 75 years old when he wrote his first, and much disputed paper on the subject, "Female Sexuality" (1931). Two years later (1933), he wrote in his second and even more criticized paper, "Femininity": "Psychology is unable to solve the riddle of femininity" (p. 116). "The development of a little girl into a normal woman is more difficult and more complicated since it includes two extra tasks, to which there is nothing corresponding in the development of a man" (p. 117).

The tasks Freud refers to represent two of his major conceptions. First, a female must come to terms with anatomy and effect a change of organ, from the clitoris to the vagina, and second, she must effect a change of object—from mother to father. It has been endlessly argued when and why a woman gives up her intense attachment to her mother in favor of her father. In the present collection of papers, some informed statements are made about these issues.

All of the case studies presented in this volume deal with such transitions from mother to father and back again, from one developmental phase to another. Highlighted are the deleterious effects when these changes do not occur. These therapists focus on them in a somewhat different way than Freud first envisioned them. Freud (1905) saw little girls as perceiving themselves as essentially male, then as castrated males (the castration complex), and not until puberty gaining a sense of vaginal awareness. Later, Freud (1923b) spoke of infantile and adult genital organization as virtually identical with regard to the object and asserted that until puberty male and female are synonymous with phallic and castrated. His phallocentric views are well known, although he was always careful to call on his female adherents to further investigate what appeared to be a mystery: female development, including sexuality.

Laura Arens Fuerstein's paper "Females in Bondage: The Early Role of Mother and Father in the Woman's Tie to Abusive Men" includes an excellent overview of Freudian and post Freudian views of such matters. Therefore, I will not subject the reader to another depiction of Freudian theory. Suffice it to say here that Freud's followers have heeded his dictum and have further investigated the mysteries of female development and sexuality.

In reading the collection of papers presented here, it becomes clear that the analysts writing them share many of Freud's convictions, but they do not think of the little girl as anything but female from birth on. For them, femininity is not achieved via a detour through masculinity (Fast, 1984; Stoller, 1977). Although their cases often demonstrate the presence of penis envy, it is not viewed as the ubiquitous developmental step Freud thought it was (Galenson & Roiphe, 1971; Roiphe & Galenson, 1981). The wish for motherhood does not always connote the wish for a penis (Glover & Mendell, 1982; Kestenberg, 1982; Kohut, 1975; Siegel, 1984). Likewise, competitiveness as a character trait in women is not always connected to penis envy or the wish to castrate men (Grossman & Stewart, 1977; Karme, 1981). Tyson (1982, 1984) demonstrates that the so-called feminine inferiority complex, masochism, and passivity are not in the least part and parcel of the character of nonneurotic women. To come full cycle to Freud's hypothesis about the lacking awareness of vaginal sensations in young females, my own clinical research (Siegel, 1984, 1988) shows that this is a pathological rather than a normal development. Despite these advances in clinical research and thinking, transference and resistance are treated in a Freudian, that is to say, an interpretive manner and receive emphasis in the case studies.

As I have already mentioned, Fuerstein's paper contains an excellent overview of a psychoanalytic developmental schema that includes the newer modifications. She uses this schema to trace the vicissitudes of her patients' stunted development. They were oedipal victors: Father was seemingly favored, mother pushed aside. Therefore, they felt that they already "had it all." In treatment, they fought therapeutic regression, free association, and the need to uncover deeper layers of the mind. In particular, they were defended against regression to the preoedipal maternal transference. In female development, anal sadistic components of toilet training need to be superseded by genital primacy so that ambivalence toward the mother is reduced. Recognition of sexual differences impedes a girl's rapprochement phase and causes her to cling to mother in pursuit of reparation and a penis. In doing so, she needs to deny her aggression against mother's body. Finally, Fuerstein sees the causes for women's masochistic relationships with their fathers and other men in the little girl's primitive idealization and attachment to mother. Fuerstein elucidates how a compromise solution for her patient is established in which the rage at mother is repressed and turned against the self in the masochistic position vis-à-vis men. However, these were not preoedipally arrested women. Rather, they had been forced by the vicissitudes of their development to use their oedipal conflict also to gratify terrifying aggressive wishes aimed at mother. In addition, being the oedipal victor allowed these women to gain the magic phallus from father in order to imagine some control over mother also. An additional important contribution in this paper is an examination of Freud's ideas about masochism as seminal to modern psychoanalytic views in which an unempathic environment is seen to skew an innate femininity toward masochism, that is, women are *not* seen as inherently castrated and/or masochistic. This paper fully and with great empathy traces one area of atypical development in women. It focuses on women who experienced their mothers as distant, cold, and dominant.

In contrast, Carolyn Celentano's "The Encapsulated Maternal Introject: In the Service of Survival" emphasizes the role of suffocating, overwhelming, and intrusive mothers who wished to control their daughters' psyches. In the case of Celentano's patients, there was a premature disruption in the mother–infant dyad. These mothers appeared unable to tolerate even a gesture that might convey the child's separateness. Despite such inauspicious beginnings, Celentano's patients were able to function with great capacity in their work lives. Like Fuerstein's patients, they had selectively identified with certain aspects of their fathers but were unable to take in much of their mothers' personality. Celentano hypothesizes this skewed development as the result of an inability by the mother to be playfully accepting of her little girl. Celentano speaks of her work as ongoing. These therapies have not yet reached their final conclusions. One wonders when and if the inevitable homosexual transferences will surface. Celentano seems willing and able to facilitate exploration of what they have missed for her patients. One wishes them well.

So far, the emphasis has been on inappropriate mothering. Ronald W. Levin presents a carefully observed and analyzed case of a woman with severe psychosomatic complaints, whose interaction with both parents was fraught with psychological peril for her. With rare tact, and without endangering the analysis, he rescues her from the medical, technological model of intervention without endangering the psychoanalytic treatment. In his paper "Somatic Symptoms, Psychoanalytic Treatment, Emotional Growth" he makes a convincing case for the hypothesis that medical, technological treatment may contribute to such patients' complicated medical course. Usually, they are women. He sees conceptualizations of technological medical caretakers as overlooking the level of emotional development of the patient and the unconscious meanings of patients' words, actions, and somatic process. As a result, such patients often do not develop emotionally; conflicts stay unresolved and actively contribute to symptoms. In contrast, the developmental, psychoanalytic approach Levin uses with sensitivity and care enables the patients to face their inner reality and defenses. This then leads to renewed psychological growth. A detailed case study of a woman with seizure and eating disorders powerfully reinforces Levin's points.

Kenneth R. King and Theodore L. Dorpat contribute one of the rare accounts of an analysis of a father–daughter incest victim, "Daddy's Girl: An Interactional Perspective on the Transference of Defense in the Psychoanalysis of a Case of Father–Daughter Incest." Pop psychology and the pseudo-scientific literature of self-help groups have recently awakened awareness in the general public of the plight of apparently numerous incest victims. In psychoanalytic circles, the question of what is significant for inner structuralization—the actual trauma or its secondary psychic elaboration—is once again being discussed. King and Dorpat point out that even though Freud (1914) shifted his focus to the interplay among actual event and trauma, fantasy and conflict, as well as constitutional factors, to the end of his life he continued to stress the pathogenic effects of childhood seduction (1917, 1918, 1933). They also point out that in the transference, the analyst immediately becomes both the abused and the abuser, setting up strong defenses that make difficulties in the transference-countertransference interplay. Most importantly, it is emphasized in this understated but highly sensitive account that incest is not simply an event. It involves an incestuous relationship in a family that denies the presence, meaning, and impact of what is happening. The young girl who is the victim cannot help but experience the greatest rage toward her mother who has allowed this to happen. King and Dorpat point out that it is essential for such patients to work through their enormous hostilities in a neutral but firm holding environment. They warn against probing questions when incest is revealed. The analyst's questions are too easily experienced by the patient as collusion and repetition of the incestuous object relationship. We are indebted to King and Dorpat for a lucid presentation that alerts the psychoanalytic practitioner to many technical pitfalls.

The paper by Florence Holland, "Aspects of Homosexuality," was written 20 years ago by a woman known for her generous lucidity in dealing with others. Although the paper never appeared in print—Holland chose to share it with only a few intimate friends—it was seminal in its effect on this writer. Holland asked the questions I later posed in my own work: Why do some women become homosexual? Why, in any given family, do some children turn out to be heterosexual, others homosexual? Holland examines this fundamental question in two case histories. Both in her daily worklife at the New York City Department of Correction's House of Detention for Women and in her practice, Holland was exposed to a large group of female homosexuals. Her vision about the etiology of female homosexuality was prophetic, not only on the social but also on the treatment level. In treating patients who were homosexual, she disavowed the techniques then in vogue: conscious manipulation and establishment of guilt in homosexual patients. Although more enlightened analysts were of the opinion that one should not, in the beginning of treatment, stop a patient from his or her homosexual aim, it was considered appropriate to interfere with the gratification experienced (Socarides, 1978). In contrast, Holland writes: "Guilt never was a reliable ally. If the thrust forward in development is absent then we have no ally; how to find that thrust forward remains the therapeutic task." Before her death, Flo entrusted this paper to me. It is my pleasure to share it with the reader.

In the second section of this volume, Susan Kavaler-Adler presents a brilliant essay about the addictiveness of certain creative endeavors by females. It is entitled "Object Relations Insights Concerning the Female as Artist. Kavaler-Adler speculates that there are gender-specific aspects to the uses and the process of artistic self-expression. She makes a strong case for this hypothesis with an examination of Emily Dickinson's life and work. She sees Dickinson's self-imposed seclusion as a way of dealing with incestuous fantasies about a father who strongly dominated any representational object form. On another level, she conceptualizes Dickinson's withdrawal as an enactment of her mother's schizoid mode. She shows that the poet's mental merger between her mother and her father made any archaic maternal form take on a masculinized veneer. Kavaler-Adler then demonstrates similar psychological events in the inner lives of other creative women, in particular a female patient in psychotherapy. A highlight of this penetrating paper is the attempt to link sociological factors and feminists' views with the material presented. Kavaler-Adler's insights are psychoanalytic, yet informed by other disciplines. They make surprisingly interesting reading.

Sidney M. Rosenblatt examines the meaning of fairy tales in the development of female sexual identity. In his paper "Thumbelina and the Development of Female Sexuality," he cogently probes the use of fairy tales to organize fantasies and to deal cognitively with forbidden subjects, such as masturbation. He finds symbols for the vagina and for the clitoris in Andersen's fairy tale, linking them with classic assumptions about female sexual development. He then raises the question of how to integrate newer insights on the development of women with the ideas of classical psychoanalytic models. He points to Bonaparte's (1953) statements that the little girl experiences birth and pregnancy as alimentary functions, thinking that birth occurs through the anus rather than through the vagina. Rosenblatt then comes up with an ingenious and practical notion: He alerts us to the fact that both oral and anal developments occur equally. He then elucidates his statements by a clinical vignette.

Penny W. Caccavo, in a densely packed paper, "The Forbidden Room: A Pair of Fairy Tales as Developmental Metaphor," presents us with a scholarly exposition of the forbidden room as the essence of the young woman's femaleness of which she must take possession in order to release her potential. Caccavo ranges far in her exploration of myth and fairy tales to cull from them the symbols for a young woman's search for bodily and psychic integrity. The struggle for separation from a dangerous maternal introject is convincingly portrayed in the copious examples from many lands and cultures Caccavo amusingly strings together. Without perhaps intending to do so, she demonstrates the ubiquitousness and accuracy of psychoanalytic theories that reach across ethnic and cultural borders. Her essay is a fitting and poetic end to a collection of papers that explores the inner world of women.

References

Bonaparte, M. (1953). *Female sexuality.* London: Imago.

Fast, I. (1984). *Gender identity.* Hillsdale, NJ: Analytic Press.

Freud, S. (1905). Three essays on the theory of sexuality. *Standard Edition, 7,* 125–243. London: Hogarth Press, 1953.

Freud, S. (1914). On the history of the psychoanalytic movement. *Standard Edition, 14,* 7–66. London: Hogarth Press, 1963.

Freud, S. (1917). Introductory lectures on psychoanalysis. *Standard Edition, 15 & 16.* London: Hogarth Press.

Freud, S. (1918). From the history of an infantile neurosis. *Standard Edition, 17,* 7–123. London: Hogarth Press, 1955.

Freud, S. (1923b). The infantile genital organization. *Standard Edition, 19,* 141–148. London: Hogarth Press, 1961.

Freud, S. (1931). Female sexuality. *Standard Edition, 21,* 225–246. London: Hogarth Press, 1961.

Freud, S. (1933). Femininity. *Standard Edition, 22,* 112–135. London: Hogarth Press, 1964.

Galenson, E., & Roiphe, H. (1971). The impact of early sexual discovery on mood, defensive organization and symbolization. *Psychoanalytic Study of the Child, 26,* 195–216. New York: Quadrangle Books.

Glover, L., & Mendell, D. (1982). A suggested developmental sequence for a preoedipal genital phase. In D. Mendell (Ed.), *Early development* (pp. 127–174). New York: S.P. Medical & Scientific Books.

Grossman, W. I., & Stewart, W. A. (1977). Penis envy: From childhood wish to developmental metaphor. In H. Blum (Ed.), *Female psychology* (pp. 193–212). New York: International Universities Press.

Karme, L. (1981). A clinical report of penis envy: Its multiple meanings and defensive functions. *Journal of the American Psychoanalytic Association, 29,* 427–446.

Kestenberg, J. (1982). The inner genital phase—prephallic and preoedipal. In D. I. Mendell (ed.), *Early female development* (pp. 81–126). New York: S.P. Medical & Scientific Books.

Kohut, H. (1975). A note on female sexuality. In P. H. Ornstein (Ed.), *The search for the self* (pp. 183–190). New York: International Universities Press, 1978.

McDougall, J. (1986). Eve's reflection: On the homosexual components of female sexuality. In H. C. Myers (Ed.), *Between analyst and patient* (pp. 213–228). Hillsdale, NJ: Analytic Press.

Roiphe, H., & Galenson, E. (1981). *Infantile origins of sexual identity.* New York: International Universities Press.

Siegel, E. V. (1984). Severe body image distortions in some female homosexuals. *Dynamic Psychotherapy, 1,* 18–28.

Siegel, E. V. (1988). *Female homosexuality.* Hillsdale, NJ: Analytic Press.

Socarides, C. W. (1978). *Homosexuality.* New York: International Universities Press.

Stoller, R. (1977). Primary femininity. In H. P. Blum (Ed.), *Female psychology* (pp. 59–78). New York: International Universities Press.

Tyson, P. (1982). A developmental line of gender identity, gender role, and choice of love object. *Journal of the American Psychoanalytic Association, 30,* 75–98.

Tyson, P. (1984). Female psychological development: An exploration of the role of the bisexual conflict. Paper presented at the fall meeting of the American Psychoanalytic Association, New York.

Females in Bondage: The Early Role of Mother and Father in the Woman's Tie to Abusive Men

Laura Arens Fuerstein, M.S.W.

> The determinants of women's choice of an object are often made unrecognizable. . . . When she turned from her mother to her father, the hostility of her ambivalent relation remained with her mother [and followed] in the train of the positive attachment and [spread] over on to the new object (Freud, 1933, pp. 132–133).

The inspiration for this paper evolved out of a common pattern noted in a number of my female patients: the use of a powerful link to an abusive male as a transference-resistance in the early treatment phase. The term "abusive" as employed here covers a wide spectrum of meaning, ranging from the emotionally controlling man who seems to have the woman "under his spell" (the Rasputin type) and ostensibly denies her a sense of self to the overtly physically injurious man.

The patients under consideration manifested several similar treatment elements. First, they were overtly heterosexual women whose neurotic attachment to a particular man was an essential part of their presenting problem and the suffering endured in that relationship was largely ego-dystonic. Second, they all had some sort of privileged relationship with their fathers and were oedipal victors in varying degrees. In most cases the fathers were favored over the mothers—in one case the patient seemed to be equally critical of both parents, but this appeared as a thin defense against guilt and rage felt toward the mother. Third, these patients all evinced a substantial resistance to regression, free association, and the deeper layers of the maternal transference for several years into treatment.

In some cases the transference neurosis began to form only when there was a notable shift in the relationship with the man. In other cases the opposite occurred: The patient seemed to need to flee from the intensity of the transference when the man in her life was out of reach or pushed aside. Overall there appeared to be a correlation between the degree of intensity in the woman's attachment to the man and the strength of the defense against the regression to the preoedipal maternal transference. Moreover, it appeared as if the female's suffering at the hands of the man acted as a buttress against a more primitive, more terrifying experience: the return to a depressed, bad maternal object with all its connotations; retaliation for expression of aggressive wishes, engulfment, loss of control, loss of self, narcissistic injury, and/or annihilation.

It is useful to highlight the female's developmental period between about 15 and 36 months when considering the origins of the aforementioned circumstances. It is during this stage that the girl faces several developmental issues that directly impact on her burgeoning femininity and establishment of primary gender identity.

An integral vicissitude of this phase requires that the anal-sadistic components of toilet training become superceded by genital primacy and ambivalence toward the mother be reduced. Another area of change at this time involves the shift from less object-directed genital play to a beginning form of masturbation, in which the girls' use of more concrete transitional objects symbolizing the mother and fantasy is introduced (Galenson & Roiphe, 1977; Marcus & Francis, 1975). A third aspect of this developmental period involves the recognition of the sexual difference. Mahler, Pine, and Bergman (1975) emphasize that this awareness impedes the girl's rapprochement and causes her to be ambivalently thrown back onto the mother in pursuit of a reparative process to counter feelings of anger around the lack of a penis.

Galenson and Roiphe (1977) highlight how this recognition of the anatomical difference is an impetus for movement toward the father but may be concomitantly impeded by excessive hostility toward the mother, particularly if preoedipal castration experiences are severe. Heimann (1952) augments this theme when she discusses the anxieties around the internalized maternal object which accentuate the girl's focus on the idealized phallus in behavior and fantasy. A need to deny her aggression toward the mother's body is a primary cause of her grievance against the mother for not bestowing her with a penis. In a sense, if she is viewed as a victim of the mother's withholding, her own hostile attacks are less guilt provoking. Tyson (1982) emphasizes that the quality of the mother-child relationship and the mother's sense of female identification will largely determine the nature of the girl's response to her awareness of the physical contrast between herself and boys.

It may be inferred from the preceding discussion that, on the one hand, there are major potential stumbling blocks in the female's effort to move away from the mother and toward the father, for example, remaining caught in the ambivalence of the toilet training stage, feeling too prohibited from masturbation and genital sexuality, or feeling too frightened about aggression toward the maternal object for her seeming denial of a penis to her daughter. Another more obvious issue involves the difficulty in leaving the exceedingly pleasant aspects of the symbiotic phase.

On the other hand, there are some compelling factors that might propel the girl toward the father. For one, she needs him to act as rescuer from the maternal engulfment and mire of ambivalence described above and as a transitional object in the struggle through the rapprochement. Abelin (1975) points to the father's unique role at this time. He writes about two aspects of the father's significance during this phase: First, he facilitates the resolution of the severe ambivalence felt toward the maternal object; second, he is a main player in the process of "early triangulation," an experience that involves the toddler's identification with the father's desire for the mother as a means of internalizing an image of her while separating from her.

Freud (1931) views the female's progression to the father as an offshoot of conflict and feelings of castration, but in the overall sense he attaches a positive and healthy coloration to the outcome—after all, she must accomplish this in order to become an oedipally functioning female and have a firm sense of female gender. He states that she also needs her father in order to find a displacement for her phallic and aggressive striving toward her mother and in order to acquire a substitute for a penis—namely a baby.

Freud (1931) adds that the female's preoedipal view of the mother as seductress (for example, when cleaning the genitals), depriver (when denying penis, love, or food), or attacking harsh superego (when prohibiting masturbation) is transferred to the father and markedly colors that relationship.

In the recent literature one of the chief modifications of Freud's theory is found in the emphasis upon the conflict-free striving toward femininity and taking the father as love object. Stoller (1977) speaks of "core gender identity," a sense of femininity rooted in physiological and emotional experiences with both parents, which occurs as an evolutionary process from birth on. Through this shifted perspective, castration and penis envy, while given value, become specific elements within a broader picture of development. Moreover, the impact of preoedipal object relationships upon these issues is brought into bold relief. Hence, the move to the father is now seen, in a healthy model, as an integral element of the rapprochement; both a catalyst and an offshoot of the separation from the mother.

While we may carry this new view in hand, Freud's (1931) recognition of the significance of the girls' preoedipal relationship with the mother in determining the complexion of her liaison with the father is worthy of note. In her classic paper, Reich (1953) writes about two types of narcissistic object choice in women: The submissive-dependent woman clings to a man throughout life and becomes subservient to him; the other type is a woman who idealizes different men and is submerged in the relationship with each of them until going on to other similar associations. Reich describes both these kinds of object choice as addictive and the result of disturbed early interactions with the mother: The "ecstatic-orgastic" fusion with the idealized male is a substitute for a primitive identification with a glorified maternal object, to compensate for the real mother's inadequacies.

Chasseguet-Smirgel (1985) writes that the father may be a "last resort," the last opportunity for the girl's establishment of a satisfying relationship with a parental figure, if there has been too much maternal frustration or other defects in the symbiotic unit. In this case the anal-sadistic and aggressive manifestation vis-à-vis the mother must be powerfully repressed, since the father/last salvation must be maintained at all costs. The result of this defensive process may be an idealization of sexuality and identification with the bad aspects of the primary object; using sex as an exploitative tool or an unconscious weapon against the man is one effect of this turn of events. A surface presentation of masochism might be one means of countering these sadistic impulses.

From a summation of the literature, one might infer that we now accept the concept of a healthy, conflict-free striving found within the female from birth, which points toward separation from the mother and progression toward the father as part and parcel of the development of femininity. However, as Chasseguet-Smirgel (1985) writes, this natural process must be facilitated by gradually dosed frustrations and positive influences within the relationship to the mother; further, the father must provide a reasonable means of projecting the mother's good aspects onto him. If this occurs, his daughter will be enabled to move through the change of object when the frustrations are felt and a nonconflictual identification with the mother will be achieved without a need to idealize the father (and other men as extensions) as a permanent compensation for the earlier deficiencies in the relationship with the mother.

In the case of the patients considered here, impediments were placed in the path leading toward separation from the mother and connection with the father. Among these were defects in the symbiotic dyad, extremes of unhealthy narcissism in the mother, which prevented her from seeing her daughter as a separate self, or major flaws in the mother's own female gender identity, which prevented enough positive identification or encouraged hatred of the father and other men. Added to these maternal inadequacies were, for example, fathers who hated women and employed special relationships with their daughters as weapons against their wives and mothers, or used seduction to control their female offspring or harm them while bolstering a deeply imbedded sense of castration in themselves.

In these cases, the man in the woman's life represents a "pseudo-change-of-object." The girl's primitive idealization and attachment to the mother remains intact through a sadomasochistic relationship with the father/other man. A compromise solution is established, in which the rage at the mother is deeply repressed and is turned against the self in the masochistic position with the man. The woman remains powerfully tied to the mother and makes an unconscious pact with her: Through the "beatings" from the father/other man, she remains tied to the mother through life and concomitantly is punished for her primitive aggressive strivings toward her; in one sense, she saves the maternal object from annihilation through a self-sacrificial act, ostensibly at the hands of the man.

Thus far, preoedipal issues have been the central focus. It should be noted that the women considered here have moved on to the oedipal phase under the weight of a powerful burden of these aforementioned elements. It is theorized here that the guilt that has been traditionally attributed to the masochistic woman's need to be abused by a sadistic man is one piece in a large picture. When discussing females with preoedipal backgrounds such as the above, taking the father from the mother is not viewed just as an achievement of oedipal rivalry; rather, it is seen as a means of gratifying terrifying, aggressive wishes aimed at the maternal object, which will annihilate her. Moreover, the act represents gratification of a wish to gain the magical phallus from the father, which has the power to provide some control over the omnipotent mother (McDougall, 1972). Hence, in addition to guilt feelings for winning father from mother, there is terror of retaliation and a paradoxical corresponding need to "hold onto her for dear life," albeit within the guise of a formidable link to a man.

Case Studies

Toby

Toby, a single young woman, came to treatment ostensibly to work out a turbulent relationship with her lover. She had just moved to the area and was insecure and ungratified in her work. She was made particularly anxious by pressures put upon her by her female supervisors. Penis envy and phallic/competitive striving were fundamental aspects of her dynamics.

The mother was a depressed housewife with whom her daughter could not positively identify; Toby had been abandoned by her at several key developmental points. The father, a successful attorney, treated his daughter as a special confidant and at critical moments in his own life, such as periods of illness or job changes, ascribed the role of wife to his daughter—in the sense of "you're the only one who can really understand."

Through reconstruction, it appeared that the father had also neglected his daughter's needs at crucial periods, but idealization seemed to prevent her from seeing this and other inadequacies found in him were brushed aside. He was the figure who provided her with a source of positive identification, and her choice of career was largely based on this modeling after him. A flagrant example of his paternal neglect could be found in his moving the family frequently for career reasons. One effect this had upon Toby was to contribute to intimacy problems with peers, and promiscuity with boys in adolescence was one defense against this. This sexualization was used until and during Toby's entrance into treatment, to ward off homosexual fears and loss of self and maintain some feeling of control of the object.

Toby had a nonidealizing positive transference during the first year of treatment. During this period, the major focus was her turbulent relationship with Phil. She felt caught in his web. She could not live without him and she felt tortured when with him. After about a year and a half Toby began to talk seriously about leaving him for a less sadomasochistic relationship. A most powerful trigger for this conscious desire was found in Phil's blatantly showing Toby photographs of old lovers in the nude—the homosexual issue lay deeply unconscious. At this time he also began to "punch her around" a bit when angry.

As Toby was able to face more of her anger toward Phil, she also was feeling closer to me, expressed the desire to increase sessions from twice to three times weekly, and several months later moved to the couch. On the night following this shift, she had the following dream, which she presented at the next session: "I am going out to sea. I look at The Statue of Liberty to guide me. Her face becomes a skull and crossbones and then she melts away." In associating to the dream, Toby had a connection to a long-repressed memory of a time when she was two and felt the emotional loss of her mother, perhaps for the first time, to a serious depression. Her maternal grandmother had just died and she felt confused and frightened. She recalled her mother going to her own room, shutting the door, and going on a crying binge which led to her first visible withdrawal from mothering.

The expected loss of the male lover/father combined with the shift to the couch, in a sense, to throw Toby back onto the preoedipal mother. In the transference, as expressed in the dream, I became that mother in the form of the Statue, a two-sided figure—one that could give her "liberty" and separation and guidance through the turbulent waters of the treatment, but could concomitantly become bad and/or disappear or be destroyed by the daughter through the very act of separating, which might be engendered. Of course, the wish to destroy the mother before she could control her withdrawal from her daughter should be noted, along with the homosexual wishes that were evoked during this period.

Following this phase, Toby exuded a great deal of anxiety and regressed with a compelling return to Phil and some acting-out of her former promiscuity through flings with several men. She presented another dream at this time: "I am on the couch and I turn over to find a dead body." Associations led to the recognition of her terror when the father became unavailable to her at the moment when she needed him most, that is, when the mother was first mired in depression and became "dead" to Toby. In the dream she kills off the transference/maternal object before she can experience the loss of her through "death" and the meaning of the flight back to Phil is revealed: She could, on one level, gain the father through him and, on a deeper level, hold on to the ephemeral mother while being beaten by her for aggressive feelings directed at her.

The dream's interpretation allowed Toby to face her fear of falling into the maternal abyss while on the couch, and her need for Phil as a defense against this was brought into bold relief. She was gradually made more able to break away from him as her masochistic stance with him became more ego-dystonic and the development of the working alliance was enhanced.

Dana

Dana had been in supportive therapy with a male therapist (Ray) for two years before entering treatment with me. She had a positive transference to him and was devastated when he left town to live elsewhere. Her presenting problem in her first therapy experience was similar to the one with me: overwhelming anxiety at unexpected times, particularly in the work setting (advertising) and frequent depressive episodes of undefined origin.

Dana had felt like the father's favorite as the second oldest child in a family with one older brother and one younger sister. When her sister was born and Dana was eleven, she felt she had lost her father to the cute, new little baby. Nevertheless, her image of the father remained as an idealized picture of a kind, nurturing man, selfless and devoted to his children. The mother, on the other hand, was viewed as the judge, the disciplinarian, and the cold one.

One of Dana's earliest memories was of being discovered in the bathroom with her first male love and childhood confidant, Alex, when they were both five. She could not remember doing anything in particular, except perhaps enacting "I'll show you mine if you show me yours." The feeling that she was "caught" in a crime by Alex's mother was very profound. This memory represented one piece of a whole picture that portrayed Dana's powerful attachment to Alex: He and she were inseparable up until the time that he moved away, when they were both about eight. Alex seems to have embodied the qualities of the good maternal object in a male figure—a replication of Dana's father and a paradigm for her choice of husband (and attachment to Ray).

Dana married a man who supplied her with a relationship similar to the ones she had with her father and Alex. This contributed to the classic split: There was little passion found in the marital bed, and other men, who were sought out for affairs, were dangerous and sadistic and provided Dana with a lurid erotic life behind the scenes. Thus, the incestuous object was not possessed in any total sense and unconscious penance was paid to the oedipal mother for the crime of wishing to replace her at the father's side (which was partially made real in this case).

During the early stages of treatment, Dana mourned the loss of

Ray. Nothing and no one could replace this therapist who had contributed to her feeling happy for the first time in many years. The anger at him for leaving her was split off, and idealization was one result.

Dana's first presented dream involved her having been raped by a man who was a composite of me and one of her lovers—she sought Ray's help, but he was unavailable to her. This dream set the stage for many other dreams and fantasies expressed in the first two years of treatment, in which I was portrayed as the punishing mother on the surface, and as the homosexual partner on a deeper level. During this phase there were no affairs and scant fantasy material involving exciting men outside the marriage.

Following this period, there was a shift to a more positive transference and development of an incipient working alliance. A move to the couch was discussed and enacted, along with increased sessions. Soon afterward, Dana's dream material was dramatically altered: Symbolism of homosexually colored interactions with me were replaced with portrayals of the couch as a coffin; I had placed her on this "gray slab" to face the responsibility of "growing up." The transference shifted from one that portrayed me as the nurturing mother to one that was composed of deprivation and punishment, meted out by a more distant maternal object. The move to the couch led to a powerful memory of being cut off from her father when Dana's sister was born. As his attentions turned toward his new baby girl, Dana was left feeling alone or thrown back onto a judgmental and aloof mother. Several affairs with elusive men ensued.

This period, characterized by a feeling of "If I cannot see you then you are not there," or by a sense of exile on the couch, was dramatized during a session when I asked about some waiting room behavior. I noticed that Dana had averted her eyes from my glance when I greeted her. She responded that she needed to do this as a protection, because if I really got a chance to look at her, I would see that she was "disgusting." When I queried further about this, she associated to a memory of being caught masturbating around the time of her sister's birth and being called "disgusting" by her mother. Following this she was able to recognize fantasies of masturbating in front of me on the couch; furthermore, the view of me as "not there" was now seen as a defense, for if I *was* there, I would catch her in the "crime" of yore. The transference now shifted back to one of a loving, all-giving mother.

Now the acting-out behavior that was triggered by the move to the couch could be clarified and formulated into something "remembered" rather than "repeated": Up until the birth of Dana's sister, she could find the good maternal object in her father and, by extension, in Alex;

the perceived loss of him, occurring at the time of the birth, led Dana to feel alone in a preoedipal sea of loss of self with the bad mother. The dilemma of needing this mother for sustenance while being driven toward separation from her was intensified due to the abandonment at the hands of her father. The origins for her adult relationships to men were now delineated: The bad mother, desperately needed and just as powerfully hated, would be split off onto the sadistic, sexually exciting lovers; the good mother would be found in a husband and Ray, an adult form of "Alex" and a supporter, a protector. In the transference, I was the good mother when I, too, could protect Dana from the onslaught of the regression to the preoedipal mother—prohibitive of masturbation and separation, while denying of love and nurturance.

When Dana could begin to recognize her need to find the archaic bad mother in her abusive lovers, she could concomitantly see her need to defend against seeing me in toto as the recipient of all of her primitive feelings and desires. Gradually she became more able to bring these elements into the transference and explore them, while the compulsive types of affairs decreased. She continued to have affairs outside the marriage for several years, but the lovers' qualities overall were less colored with sadism and control issues.

Discussion

In any discussion of a relationship in which it appears that one party seeks out abuse at the hands of another, the role of masochism requires attention. Freud views masochism from varied perspectives throughout his work. He sees it as an integral part of perversion, in which satisfaction is attained through physical or emotional suffering (1905). He describes it as a reversal of sadism, in which an active stance toward the object shifts to a passive one (1915). In "The Wolf Man" (1914) and "A Child is Being Beaten" (1919), he notes the role of guilt felt toward the parent of the same gender and how it melds with the expression of sexual love feelings experienced with either parent in the act of being beaten. Freud later delineates three categories of masochism: erotogenic, moral, and feminine. "Erotogenic" involves the "lust of pain," "moral" is rooted in a sense of guilt, and "feminine" is related specifically to the woman's passive role in intercourse (1924).

If we consider the varied areas of focus in Freud's study of the subject, at times it appears we are dealing with general concepts (i.e., "erotogenic"); at other times we are provided with greater detail regarding the roots of a masochistic stance. For example, Freud painstakingly describes the Wolf Man's process of regression to a masochistic position, which is colored with passivity and anal-sadistic elements, as due to incestuous guilt and a need to retain the love of his father. He writes: "By bringing his naughtiness forward he was trying to force punishments and beatings out of his father, and in that way to obtain from him the masochistic sexual satisfaction that he desired . . . in accordance, moreover, with the motives which underlie masochism, this beating would also have satisfied his sense of guilt" (1914, p. 28).

In attempting to gain a more comprehensive understanding of the cases under discussion, we can incorporate some of Freud's seminal ideas on the subject of masochism and see where they require modification and/or embellishment. Three areas demand immediate attention: first, the concept of "female masochism"; second, the exclusion of a discussion of the influence of the early mother/child relationship upon the future relationships of the masochist—in this case, the focus is on the woman; third, the role of the father.

Freud's definition of female masochism is based upon his view of the woman as having an inherent sense of castration and need to shift to passivity in the development of her femininity (1933). With our contemporary appreciation of the concept of core gender identity, our perspective on female masochism modifies Freud's stance. If we accept the idea that the girl enters the world with an innate capacity for the development of femininity, which requires the proper greenhouse for its flowering, masochism might be seen largely as the result of environmental skewing, rather than part and parcel of her womanhood. One other way to look at it is to say that a woman's genital achievement, a capacity to allow and take pleasure in being penetrated by a man, need not equate with a masochistic position.

Freud's theories on masochism, as he noted himself in his later years, do not pay sufficient attention to the preoedipal relationship to the mother (Panken, 1983). One offshoot of this omission might be found in the frequent assumption that a woman seeks beatings from a man because of her oedipal guilt. While such guilt may be integral in this case, the preoedipal precursors described in the preceding sections of this paper play a significant role in the coloration of the oedipal phase and often underlie the manner in which the guilt is evidenced.

When Freud writes about the father's role in the establishment of a masochistic stance in his child (as in the case of "The Wolf Man" or "A Child is Being Beaten"), he is considering either an image or an enactment of a father who spanks his child. The focus here is modified and therefore requires an augmented understanding of the father's role. First, we are speaking of the child in the adult masochist; second, the concern is specific to women; and third, the masochism may be experienced in an abstract emotional sense.

With the aforementioned discussion in hand, we may now ask: What is peculiar to the constellation of developmental events in the lives of these patients under consideration, which leads to the retainment of the bad maternal object through paternal beatings of an emotional and/or physical nature? The answer is based on informed speculation and is meant to lead to further study for validation or refutation.

The mothers in these cases are described by their daughters in varying degrees as distant, cold, strict, and the dominant force in the family. In no case has there been an adequate amount of physical affection between mother and daughter. The mother's sense of her female identity appears flawed in a significant way in many of these cases. Memories of being prohibited from masturbation at an early age, through severe chastisement by the mother, and of rigid toilet training techniques applied too early in development are common in these patients.

The stage is set then, in the preoedipal years, for these daughters to ultimately look to the father, not only as a rescuer from the symbiotic dyad or a facilitator of the rapprochement (a position he takes in the "average expectable environment"), but as his daughter's salvation —a hoped-for anchor in a flood of desperation. It might be inferred that a father with so much invested in him needs a great degree of ego strength and a finely tuned capacity to reach out to his daughter to bolster her feminine strivings, without crossing over into the realm of manipulation, seduction, or betrayal. A corollary would be that his relationship with his own mother and other caretaking women during childhood is crucial in the establishment of this balanced relationship with his daughter.

In the cases considered, it appears that this equilibrium is unattainable. Through reconstruction, it is revealed that the fathers of these women harbor an unconscious rage toward their own mothers, which require powerful repressive devices (in several of these scenarios the paternal grandmothers had died when their sons were rather young and elder female siblings raised their younger brothers in harsh ways, often acting out their own resentments for having motherhood prematurely foisted upon them). When these boys (the future fathers of my patients) become men, they marry women who represent the split-off idealized dead mother toward whom anger cannot be directly expressed. The anger is manifested in the covert or overt seduction of their daughters—through the "special" relationship, the abandoning mother is acquired and abandoned in turn. The wife is shut out emotionally and the daughter is ultimately double-crossed.

While the surface coloration of the father/daughter relationship under discussion reflects intimacy and validation of the girl's feminine strivings, the deeper layers evince an envy and resentment of her gender. The daughter's ultimate adult solution, found in the masochistic relationship with her husband or lover, is a two-edged sword (sometimes both literally and figuratively). One side of the masochism represents the reversal of sadistic impulses aimed at the father for his unconscious denial and envy of her femininity. Because she so desperately needs him, her aggression toward him must be kept hidden at all costs. She remains connected to him through a charade of femininity, a replication of the childhood relationship with him—she is ostensibly a fine lover, her father's special sexual mate in intercourse. Also worthy of note is the disguise of the deeper homosexual issues provided by this type of relationship with men—a subject which is beyond the scope of this paper.

The other aspect of the self-directed abuse reflects the experience of being thrown back onto the preoedipal mother due to the feeling of betrayal at the father's hands. The maltreatment represents the most powerful aspect of the early relationship with the mother. In Kleinian terms, the primitive infantile aggressive impulses are turned against the self as the maternal introject is retained (a bad object is better than no object). Concomitantly there is atonement for oedipal guilt rooted in the nearly successful effort to wrest the father from the mother. In a sense, the so-called oedipal victor must once again pay a high intrapsychic price for winning what seems, for a fleeting moment, to be the spoils of victory.

Conclusion

As Freud and others have emphasized, a balanced view of any piece of pathological behavior requires a backdrop of normality, or at least one that, as nearly as possible, approaches intrapsychic health. In line with this thinking, our perspective on female patients who are ostensibly bound to sadistic men is gained through the vision of a girl's normal development. In simple terms, she must move from mother to father to the outside world in order to become a healthy, genitally functioning woman. In more technical terms, she must enjoy an adequate symbiosis with her mother, in which there is a facilitation of her striving to separate and provision of a positive female identification found in her mother. If these elements exist without an excess of feelings of fusion and engulfment, she will naturally move on to her father, who is seen both as a stepping stone through the rapprochement and an object of her love. As an adult sexual woman, she can then make a relationship with men who are more or less appropriate for her and can gratify her needs for an intimate relationship incorporating both tender and sexual feelings.

While this model may appear simplistic and unattainable in toto, it illuminates the skewing in the developmental journeys of the women in the vignettes presented above. In these cases, there is the quality of an addiction in the relationship of the women to their men. The clinging to the man out of desperation and at almost all costs resembles an infant reaching out for a nipple after a long period of painful hunger. This sadistic man does not represent a choice made at the culmination of a natural progression; rather, he is a vehicle for a powerful defensive process. If he is cast off, the abuse received from him, which is experienced as painful yet strangely controllable, is traded in for a worse agony, namely, that of loss of self or feared annihilation of the maternal object.

What are the treatment elements that might permit such a defensive process to be altered so that the healing effects of the working through may be actualized? In the vignettes presented, it is noted that some shift in the resistance occurred, that is, some of the acting-out with the male figure in the outside world abated when the love for the preoedipal maternal object could be reawakened without the threat of the original terrors being evoked. In theory, the women patients under discussion should be able to choose more appropriate lovers and/or husbands in the future, after the maternal transference is more fully worked through. Some of their own sadism, if permitted free reign in the transference with the mother, should become conscious enough so that the need to disguise it so well through the masochistic stance with the men in their lives may dissipate.

What of the father in this treatment scenario? It is clear to us from the model of normal development that his role as a bridge from the preoedipal mother through separation-individuation to the outside world is crucial. Yet, in the treatment setting, and perhaps even more so with a female analyst, it is often difficult to delineate the paternal transferences and to see them as having a definition outside that of the maternal transferences. Part of this lack of clarity may be related to the shift in the analytic literature over the years from an emphasis upon the oedipal stage to one on the preoedipal years. An inherent aspect of this evolution seems to have been a decreased interest in the father (in contrast with Freud, who gave him too central a role in his studies).

While, in recent years, the pendulum has swung back somewhat to an increased focus upon the role of the father in development, his unique place in the treatment room, particularly in the transference, often seems more blurred or less understood than that of the mother. Even the terms we are so familiar with at this point, which refer to aspects of the preoedipal mother, reflect this contrast in emphasis. This "maternal language" has not only a vocabulary of many words, but one that provides wide-ranging yet specific meanings: What "paternal language" counterparts are there for "holding environment," "the good mother," "the bad mother," "good breast," "bad breast," "withholding mother," "good enough mother," "proper weaning?" While there are many terms related to the father in a clinical sense, they do not seem to be as much a part of the matrix of the analytic vocabulary as those evoking maternal issues.

Of course, the significance of the "preoedipal mother stage" is not debated here, and in fact, the subject warrants continued and expansive study. What is being underscored is that in the clinical realm, this early mother often seems viewed within a vacuum, outside of which lies the father, when in reality we know that the father's presence is felt by the child at a very young age, perhaps from birth on (Temeles, 1983). From the cases discussed it is evident that the parents' roles interface with one another; in a sense each takes a turn at being an abettor to the other engaging in a neurotic love pattern with the daughter.

During the early treatment phase, the patients considered transferences to me were infiltrated with feelings about the "seductive father," the "rescuing father," the "facilitating father," etc. Gradually, more of these paternal transferences developed in the progression from the mother/analyst to the outside world of men. The conceptualization of both sets of transference reactions, as they act individually and weave together in the earlier and later stages of treatment of similar patients, might provide the truest reflection of the developmental move from "mother to father to the outside world."

References

Abelin, E. (1975). Some further observations and comments on the earliest role of the father. *International Journal of Psychoanalysis, 56,* 293–302.

Chasseguet-Smirgel, J. (1985). *Female sexuality: New psychoanalytic views.* London: Maresfield Library.

Freud, S. (1905). Three essays on the theory of sexuality. *Standard Edition, 7,* 136–248.
Freud, S. (1914). From the history of an infantile neurosis. *Standard Edition, 17,* 7–124.
Freud, S. (1915). Instincts and their vicissitudes. *Standard Edition, 14,* 111–140.
Freud, S. (1919). A child is being beaten. *Standard Edition, 17,* 175–204.
Freud, S. (1924). The economic problem of masochism. *Standard Edition, 19,* 157–172.
Freud, S. (1931). Female sexuality. *Standard Edition, 21,* 223–246.
Freud, S. (1933). Femininity. *Standard Edition, 22,* 112–135.
Galenson, E., & Roiphe, H. (1977). Some suggested revisions concerning early female development. In H. P. Blum (Ed.), *Female sexuality* (pp. 29–57). New York: International Universities Press.
Heimann, P. (1952). A contribution to the re-evaluation of the Oedipus complex—the early stages. *International Journal of Psychoanalysis, 33,* 84–92.
Mahler, M., Pine, F., & Bergman, A. (1975). *The psychological birth of the human infant.* New York: Basic Books.
Marcus, I. M., & Francis, J. J. (1975). *Masturbation from infancy to senescence.* New York: International Universities Press.
McDougall, J. (1972). Primal scene and sexual perversion. *International Journal of Psychoanalysis, 53,* 372–384.
Panken, S. (1983). *The joy of suffering.* New York: Jason Aronson.
Reich, A. (1953). Narcissistic object choice in women. *Journal of the American Psychoanalytic Association, 1,* 22–44.
Stoller, R. J. (1977). Primary femininity. In H. P. Blum (Ed.), *Female sexuality* (pp. 59–78). New York: International Universities Press.
Temeles, M. S. (1983). The infant: A socially competent individual. In J. D. Call, E. Galenson & R. L. Tyson (Eds.), *Frontiers of infant psychiatry* (pp. 178–187). New York: Basic Books.
Tyson, P. (1982). A developmental line of gender identity, gender role, and choice of love object. *Journal of the American Psychoanalytic Association, 30,* 61–86.

The Encapsulated Maternal Introject: In the Service of Survival

Carolyn Celentano, A.C.S.W.

During a recent discussion with a group of female professionals, the conversation turned to an analysis of their professional lives. Each of the four attributed their success in their work lives to their fathers, adding that their mothers had not been suitable role models for them. Fathers were perceived as having been intelligent, ambitious, and exciting, while mothers were experienced as having been suffocating, overwhelming, and intrusive.

My thoughts turned to some of my female patients, whom I had heard voice the same sentiments. The first temptation is to regard these comments and feelings as oedipal derivatives, evidence of competitive feelings toward mother, and wishes to devalue her to "make way for daughter." My sense, however, is that this may be deceptively simple, and a further look may be required.

Listening to my patients over time, I have been struck by how many of them appear to have gross deficits in the area of the mother/daughter relationship, yet function in a high capacity in their work lives. What is impaired, as is obvious early in treatment, is their interpersonal relationships. They appear to have been able to "take in" some aspects of mother. They are feminine in appearance, not overtly homosexual, and have a reasonable degree of ego strength. There appears to be evidence of early nurturing by mother. What they were not able to do, it seems, is identify with mother during the crucial preoedipal period, when little girls must give up their dream of having father to themselves and look to mother for a female identity. This is the time when mother conveys to her daughter that she finds her attractive, desirable, and worthy of being loved. It goes without saying that if mother has not experienced this in relation to her own mother, she will not be able to do it. It is like a preliminary to the "courtship" that goes on between father and daughter later as preparation for the more mature man-woman relationship to follow. There is a courtship period between mother and daughter also, in which the little girl "tries out" being the sexual, seductive, and "wooing" mother. This presupposes an earlier period of "playfulness" between the two, a "dialoguing," which is part of the "good enough fit." I will return to the theme of "playing" at a later point.

Theoretical Considerations

Kestenberg (1957) explores the "seemingly divergent" theories of the role of the vagina in early development. She sees struggles between mechanisms leading to the rejection of the vagina and enhancing penis envy, as well as ways and means of early preparation for the feminine role as traced back to childhood. How one resolves these struggles, and with that the "full acceptance of the total genital region," will be dependent on one's ability to accept and use one's bisexuality without fear or guilt.

In her discussion of the "early maternal stage of development" (the anal stage), Kestenberg describes the little girl's use of doll play to master what she feels as "attacks on the inside," as a result of abdominal pressures that had been experienced as "overwhelming to the ego." This, before sphincter control helps her to master the "attacker." She equates her "baby" with this unrelieved pressure and the baby-genital equation is born. She now acquires "some degree of illusory control over the vagina," through externalizing the vaginal impulses upon the "baby," thereby "dominating" the baby/feelings. Mother, who according to Kestenberg is the "symbolic successor" of these abdominal pressures, is needed to play the role of baby frequently, while the little girl acts the part of mother (persecutor, harasser) with variations on the theme and roles shifting. For Kestenberg, the anal-sadistic fight with mother is the "prototype" of the fight for independence.

I find Kestenberg's formulations and understanding of the subtleties involved in this early interaction fascinating and comprehensive, as well as pertinent to appreciating some of the underpinnings of female development. What I am particularly taken with is the role of mother in shaping her daughter's sense of femaleness as she allows herself to be "used" in this process. What is required of mother is that she "be" (in what I would understand as her own femaleness), and that she allow her daughter to "be." She must allow her young daughter to cast her in the role necessary to play out what sometimes amounts to an anal-sadistic battle on daughter's part. For daughter, the issue is one of freedom, and in her play, she attempts to master feelings involving separation and autonomy.

Winnicott speaks of the "potential space," wherein he says, "the question of separation does not arise because in the potential space between the baby and mother, there appears the creative playing that arises naturally out of the relaxed state" (Davis & Wallbridge, 1991, p. 169).

He speaks of the mother's "female element potential," which he says "enhances her capacity to identify with the female element in her boy or girl baby (Davis & Wallbridge, 1991, p. 90). This sets the tone for what he calls the "experience of being." Without the capacity on mother's part to "allow" her baby the sense of identity arising out of the continuity of "being," "doing" and "being done to" are not experiences within the competence of the ego, do not carry the "feeling of real," and cannot "be the basis for creative living."

In *Boundary and Space* Winnicott's "potential space" is referred to as "the place where meaningful communication takes place . . . the common ground in affectionate relationships where instinct tension is not a main feature . . . communication comes about through mutuality of experience" (Davis & Wallbridge, 1981, p. 65). For Ogden (1986), writing about Winnicott's ideas, it refers to "an intermediate area of experiencing that lies between fantasy and reality . . . including the play space" (p. 205). He sees "potential space" originating in what he calls a "potential physical and mental space *between* mother and infant" (p. 205). And in Winnicott's own words, "Potential space both joins and separates the infant . . . and the mother (object)" (Ogden, 1986, p. 205). He says:

> This is the paradox I accept and do not attempt to resolve. The baby's separating out of the world of objects from the self is achieved only through the absence of a space between (the infant and mother). The potential space being filled is in the way that I am describing . . . (i.e., with illusion, with playing and with symbols). (Ogden, 1986, p. 205)

Winnicott distinguishes between imagination and fantasy saying, "In the absence of potential space, there is only fantasy; within potential space, imagination can develop" (Ogden, 1986, p. 214). For him, "symbols originate in potential space." In the beginning, when there is a "good enough fit," he says, symbols are unnecessary. Within the mother-infant unit, mother, as recognizable to an observer, "exists only in the fulfillment of need that the infant does not yet recognize as need" (p. 214).

Recognizing that some degree of failure to empathize is necessary for the infant to recognize needs as wishes, both Khan (1974) and Ogden (1986) speak to "repeated impingement" or "cumulative trauma," seeing this at one end of a wide variety of causes of "premature disruption" of the unity of mother/infant. One of the results I find applicable to my patients is what Ogden sees as the collapse or limitation of the dialectic of reality and fantasy, with collapse in the direction of reality, reality used as a defense against fantasy. Here imagination is foreclosed. He explains:

> When a relatively unrestricted psychological process has been established, a little girl playing house is both a little girl and a mother, and the question of which she is, never arises. Being a little girl who feels loved by her mother (in reality) makes it safe for her to borrow what is her mother's (in fantasy) without fear of retaliation or fear of losing herself in her mother, and, as a result, disappearing as a separate person. Being a mother (in fantasy) gives the little girl access to and use of all the richness of the cultural, familial, and personal symbols (e.g., in relation to what it means to be a female, a mother, and a daughter) that have been consciously and unconsciously conveyed in the course of *real* experience with her mother, father and others.
>
> On the other hand, if the little girl is *only* a little girl, she is unable to play; she is unable to imagine and will be unable to feel she is alive in any sense. Such a situation arises when reality must be used as a defense against fantasy. (Ogden, 1986, p. 219)

In the case of my patients, a number of factors appeared to contribute to a premature disruption in the mother-infant unit, eliminating the possibility for "dialectical process" to occur. There was no "playing" as I understand the term and no "playfulness." Mother was either depressed or, in the case of a patient I will discuss, bordering on psychotic, or struggling with such a weak sense of her own femaleness that she needed her daughter to provide a more complete sense of her own self (a tremendously deficient one). Daughters then experienced mothers as either toxic, suffocating, or destructively intrusive. Mother, it appears, could not tolerate even a gesture that might convey her child's sense of separateness.

The Encapsulated Maternal Introject

In attempting to understand what I was seeing with my patients, I began to think about introjects. It appeared that during the early period of introjections, part/mother was allowed in by the child. Splitting would be necessary to ensure that the "bad," "toxic" parts of mother would not be absorbed. It is as though my patients were able to allow some parts of the maternal introject to be incorporated, but in a sense, suspended the rest, the not so "palatable" as it were, to be assimilated at a later time (provided the opportunity presented itself). I conceptualize this as an encapsulated maternal introject. By keeping the harmful parts of mother at bay in this way, daughters were able to continue to grow psychically, but with some considerable deficits, which I will discuss. She is forced to turn prematurely to father as a means of survival and takes from him her sense of identity, which leads to all kinds of later acting out. She is able, usually after a tumultuous adolescence, to regain some sense of self (however fragile) and, at least in the case of my patients, creates a decent professional life, having "used" those parts of father (and mother) she needed to survive. Her sense of self, as might be expected, however, is a shaky one.

These patients, incidentally, have a degree of pathology that appears to be more severe than that of the neurotic patient. Although they function well in their professional lives, there is a vague quality about them, calling to mind Helene Deutsch's (1965) "as if" patients (Khan, 1974, p. 243). There is a stated feeling of isolation from others. It is hard, in initial sessions, to determine just what the problem is, but the patients' concreteness is immediately evident. In spite of what, by their reports are "good enough lives," there is an emptiness about them. It is only after they have been in treatment awhile (provided they stay) that one gets a sense of how the difficulty in that early mother/child relationship is responsible for what we are seeing.

Ferenczi (1909) was the first to use the term "introject." The term has been debated as to its use as a verb and its ties to incorporation and identification. Giovacchini (1975) uses the term to refer to "experiences and objects that have become part of the ego but have a distinguishable structure that sets them apart from the rest of the ego" (p. 166). He believes that once they are integrated as "adaptive techniques" into the ego system, they become assimilated and essentially lose their status as introjects. For him, introjects are instrumental in the formation of the ego, not just for a coherent identity, but for starting the process that leads toward a "unified ego organization."

This allows the psyche to deal with instinctual pressures as well as those of the outer world. The maternal introject becomes the "core" around which other adaptive experiences develop. If the introject is traumatic or disruptive, it is not assimilated into the ego.

It was in thinking about my patients and their encapsulated maternal introjects that I was reminded of Giovacchini's "frozen introjects." He cites cases of two men, in his work on character disorders, who appeared to "freeze" their maternal introjects following early traumatic parent loss. To have hypercathected the lost love objects would have been overwhelmingly destructive. This "freezing" allowed them to defend against their own underlying rage, but in the process, their productivity was "paralyzed," Correspondingly affected was the acquisition of adaptive techniques: tasks of the ego. It is significant to note that even before the trauma of parental loss early in life, the maternal introjects of these men were not particularly functional. They had been experienced as assaultive and destructive, and by "freezing" the introject, they had managed to repress or deny the destructive image. This in turn led to what Giovacchini sees as a "fixed ego state."

"I found Giovacchini's (1975) understanding and description of the introjection process extremely helpful in working with my own patients. He describes the "progressive developmental sequence" from the symbiotic phase as follows:

> As the diffuse but harmonious mother-ego fusion undergoes differentiation, the internalized mothering experience becomes delineated and develops into what could be considered an introject. Within the ego, boundaries form around the maternal representation. These boundaries mark the beginning of the psychic separation of the child from his mother. . . .
>
> As the maternal introject is increasingly consolidated, the child's behavior becomes organized and goal-directed. His play activity usually includes a problem situation that he has to resolve: often the problem is the actual or anticipated separation from the mother. . . .
>
> The object relationship with the mother is functional. That which is introjected is operational. The mother represents nurture and care, and the child's representation of her reflects her adaptive significance. As the maternal introject is "absorbed," it helps to structuralize various ego systems such as the integrative and executive systems. The executive apparatus expands and acquires further techniques of mastery by incorporating the functional maternal introject. The latter is no longer a distinct entity but has become a modality. (p. 166)

What I am positing in the case of my patients is an introject that was not able to be absorbed into the rest of the personality. For some of the reasons touched on, including the ego's attempts to defend itself against the experience of an overwhelming, destructive maternal introject, that introject is, I believe, suspended in what I have come to conceptualize as an encapsulated form, to be assimilated, hopefully, in the analytic process.

Clinical Illustrations

I would like to illustrate, with some examples from my practice, several patients who evidence a certain type of concreteness I believe is indicative of faulty organization, which Giovacchini (1975) refers to as an "ego defect." Whether this is due to a need to defend themselves against intolerable ego states, or a lack of development of the capacity to use abstract thinking or symbolization, I believe the rigidity in their secondary processing is related to their inability to have absorbed the early maternal introject, except, in part, into the personality.

Rene

Rene, a 40-year-old married woman, has been in treatment for about seven months. She is a teacher of home economics in a high school. She came in around issues related to her mother's deteriorating health. Mother has Alzheimer's disease and is in a nursing home. Father is still alive as well as a brother, several years younger, who is married with two children.

Rene is fearful that like mother, she will "go crazy." She describes a mother who always seemed "out of it." Mother appears to have suffered tremendous deficits in her own early parenting, and may have had some organic damage as well. At any rate, the result for the patient was a critical, disapproving parent, who discouraged her from having friends. Mother attempted to control the patient's every move. She recalls once playing with a schoolmate after class at home and, upon father's return that evening, mother complaining that the patient had "ignored her all day." She did not repeat the experience.

Mother seemed to be lacking in the basic skills necessary to run a home. She did cook but was not able to handle money, for example, so father took over. A shopping trip would turn into a disaster on the few occasions when mother and daughter attempted it. According to Rene, her mother did not seem to understand the rudimentary mechanics of shopping and would become nervous and agitated in the process. She said outlandish things. She once told her daughter that as a child, she (mother) had "had a nerve removed" during some dental work and had suffered a nervous breakdown as a result. According to Rene, this was not just a mother trying to explain a complicated situation to a young child, but an example of mother's "literalness."

Rene had few friends and no boyfriend until she went away to college, something she secretly dreamed about doing for years. She married her only boyfriend at age 21. She "copied" the other girls at school to learn how to dress and act. She tells a story of listening to them talk about missing their mothers and being "astounded" that they could feel that way. She had "absolutely no sense" of what that felt like. She has been married for 19 years to her husband and they are childless (although they raise pedigree dogs which they treat like children). She had decided years ago not to have children as a result of her childhood, which she does not see as having been particularly unhappy. She and her husband travel, read a good deal, and enjoy socializing in small groups. Recently, Rene told me that while reading, she will frequently query her husband as to whether or not he "feels" like the characters in the stories they are reading. In this way, she says, they "learn" what it is people "feel" in particular situations.

In a poignant early session, Rene brought in an old picture of her family to "show me what they looked like." A second picture showed her at about two years of age with mother holding her on her lap. Rene pointed to it saying, "You see, she did hold me." She seemed to need to quell her own feelings that mother had not loved her enough. She is very anxious about the relationship with mother, whom she visits twice weekly in the nursing home. She visits, she says, because it wouldn't be "nice" not to. She feels "disloyal" saying bad things about mother. They were taught "not to show emotions ever."

Father was her role model. Although there are suggestions that he had a serious drinking problem for several years and an eating disorder as well, it was he who "kept the family going." Rene saw him as "intelligent," "humorous," and "ambitious." She very much identifies with him. Father worked two jobs and, when he was home, kept himself busy with projects it sometimes took him years to complete. Nevertheless, he was clearly her inspiration to go to school and get a master's degree. (She has two.)

Rene's concreteness is evidenced in a particular way. She brings "lists" of what she wishes to discuss in session. She will ask me if she should "start" and will literally read from the list. Sometimes it is a memory she has jotted down; sometimes it is a reference to an event or person. Frequently she will make a list, for example, under "Angry Feelings," which she will read rather mechanically. Free association is an unknown to her. She becomes flustered and unnerved if I ask her to say what comes to mind.

In spite of this, Rene is intelligent, cultured, and feminine in appearance. She has "learned" how to appreciate art history, travel, and the "finer things in life." What she did not learn from mother, she has managed to "take in" from other sources. While father was her model for her education and professional aspirations, she was not able to get from him the sense of herself as a woman necessary to feel complete in terms of female identity. She has conflicts in the area of female relationships. She has had several long-standing relationships with women which seemed to end badly. From what I can ascertain, her relationships are intense and the other friend seems to "back off." My sense is that she does not know how "to be" in a relationship with a woman. It is still very early in the treatment, and Rene is beginning to "relax" to the point where we can very tentatively begin to explore some of her "feelings" about women. For purposes of this writing, I am making a case for a severe deficit in the early mother/daughter relationship, which I am attempting to understand through the process of introjection and the corresponding relationship to ego adaptation or lack of.

Ellen

Ellen is a 34-year-old woman who has been in treatment about two years. She is married with two small children. She teaches music at a local high school, specifically string instruments. She plays cello, violin, and piano. She is attractive, feminine in appearance, and "very concrete." She was referred originally by a physical therapist who had been treating her for very painful bursitis of the shoulder. The therapist was male and she felt "very close" to him. The sense I have is that he began to be uncomfortable with the relationship and was not able to handle his own feelings.

The patient is the oldest of three. She has a brother about 15 months younger and a sister four years her junior. Her brother functions marginally, having had several years of difficulty with drug and alcohol abuse. Her sister is a heroin addict who is married to an addict and lives in a furnished room. They have a 15-year-old son who lives essentially on the streets.

Ellen's parents divorced when she was 14 years of age after many stormy years of marriage. Mother was stricken with polio when Ellen was an infant and conceived her second child while she was in and out of an iron lung. There was great chaos during the early years and mother, an alcoholic, retired to her room and drank more and more as the years went by. Care of the children fell to father and his relatives.

Father was a high school principal. He took care of Ellen and apparently his wife as well. After the third child, the marriage appeared to deteriorate further, and, from the patient's accounts, mother had less and less to do with parenting. Memories that are accessible have to do with father cooking, shopping, and generally being "mommy" for Ellen, while brother lived off and on with family members, and younger sister, to some extent, shuffled between family members. Other memories are of when mother was "available" to her.

The divorce, after which father immediately remarried, was devastating for Ellen. She lived for a time with father and his new wife, where, according to her, she could do "nothing right." She was expected to care for her stepsiblings, one of whom was retarded. She did not get along with her stepmother. She remembers a period of adolescent despair, where for a time she used drugs to counter depression and anger. "No one seemed to notice or care." Father, who had been her anchor, was no longer available. She had talent in the area of music, she found, and with the help of some of her teachers was able to get a scholarship to college. She felt as though her father and stepmother couldn't wait to be rid of her.

At college, Ellen met a fellow musician, whom she lived with and eventually married. She remembers college as "the loneliest of times." Her husband is a rather nonambitious fellow who appears to be a counter to her perfectionistic ways. He seems to go from project to project—very much the adolescent in search of an identity. He has his own rage and infuriates his wife repeatedly by passively, and sometimes not so passively, provoking her. He never lives up to her standards, standards she is also not up to. The marriage is often unsatisfying to Ellen, yet she "needs" to be involved in the acting out that goes on between the two of them.

Ellen has great difficulty in her personal relationships. She has few friends. She exhausts herself with a rigorous schedule teaching and caring for her two children, in addition to extracurricular activities which involve music. She "knows" she is angry but "does not know what to do about it." Sometimes she becomes so enraged that she fears she will "lose it" and become "totally crazy."

Our work has been difficult and painstaking due to Ellen's concreteness and intellectualization. Interpretations often fall far short of the mark, and we are left trying to understand in ways that defy traditional ways of analytic working. My sense is that Ellen was not able to "take in" very much of this very disturbed mother and had to turn to father for her survival. He was not only the person who "mothered" her earlier in life, but was the primary role model for her throughout. He is not without deficits, one being his capacity to intellectualize and concretize rather than deal with what must have been some overwhelming feelings of his own. For Ellen, this has been costly. Although she is feminine in appearance, she must "work" hard, for example, at her own mothering. There are areas that are not "natural." Everything she does she must work at and do to perfection. A recent example comes to mind.

Ellen wanted a family portrait taken and, for the occasion, took the day off from work (a most unusual event). She shopped for clothes for herself and her two daughters, five and 18 months old. She color coordinated her outfit with theirs, as well as with the colors in the living room where the portrait would hang. She rented a tuxedo for her husband and asked him to match his tie and cummerbund to her color scheme. (He ended up with the "wrong" colors; his customary way of provoking and disappointing her.) She scheduled a morning appointment with a photography studio so that the children would not be cranky. (The day was a disaster for reasons I will not expound on, but which can be gleaned from what I have said about their dynamics.) It is as though by "making a perfect picture," the reality might be obscured. It also appears to represent a wish to have a "natural" family, something Ellen never experienced. The picture, as I think about it, is like the encapsulated introject in the sense that something gets suspended or stilled in time or space. If the "real" picture (whole introject) were to come to life, Ellen would be overwhelmed, "go crazy." It becomes necessary to "pretend" that things are as perfect as they would appear in the family portrait, but too much energy must be expended to keep this "perfect picture" look to things. Like Rene, the previous patient discussed, pictures become substitutes for what was missed in reality.

Lela

The third patient who comes to mind, Lela, is a 40-year-old teacher. (It may not be accidental that all three women chose to teach, although in different subject areas.) Lela is a reading teacher who came to treatment two years ago as a result of her husband leaving her and their two adolescent children. She has spent the past two years dealing with some very painful issues around separation and abandonment, as well as learning to negotiate realities such as finances and parenting alone. Her former husband, a pediatrician, has since remarried.

Lela is the youngest of two siblings. Her brother, several years younger, is married, childless, and quite disturbed. He has a long history of drug and alcohol abuse.

Initially, Lela presented a picture of an early father who was violent and abusive to "everyone but her." Mother was "good." Brother was "OK" but somewhat "spoiled." Exploration of her marital history suggested that her husband had also been quite "spoiled" and, in fact, quite abusive emotionally. He appears to be a narcissistic man with little capacity for self-reflection, something Lela was aware of before the marriage. Like many young women, she believed she could "change him." What was evident even early on was that she was familiar with this kind of emotional abuse.

After some months of some very concrete exchanges, I began to get a picture of Lela's mother, who was ambitious for her and pushed her into marrying a man who would be financially successful, in spite of other obvious shortcomings. Mother has absolutely no ability to understand or empathize with her daughter's pain, and it is unlikely she ever did. When Lela was a little girl, if mother was displeased with her, she simply wouldn't speak to her for days. Often, in our sessions, Lela would respond to a question on my part with another question, almost sounding "dull," as if she couldn't comprehend what I was asking. My question was generally in the form of some family history or connection, and Lela would become defensive and angry and respond very concretely with a question along the lines of "What do you mean?" This would be in response to the simplest query on my part. Eventually I learned that Lela felt that I was being critical or disapproving, as she had experienced mother often, and that her "dullness" was really a defensive maneuver to "keep me out," and keep herself "safe" from my/mother's anger and her own.

What also became clearer to me was that, in spite of father's violent temper and outbursts, he was more trustworthy and reliable to the young Lela. She is a long way from working analytically, but we are beginning to explore some of the roots of her mistrust of women and "openness" to men, in spite of their hurtfulness.

This last idea was graphically illustrated recently when the patient developed a sexually transmitted disease after dating several men. We had been discussing (not easily) the idea of her not using precautions in the face of all of the dangers of unprotected sex. Again, there was this kind of "dullness" to her response, as if the facts of sexual disease were unknown to her. This, from a woman who teaches adolescents, raised some questions. We were able to determine that there is a "denial" on her part of the reality of the danger she subjects herself to, as well as some acting out, to be sure. What we were able to determine as well is that the "hurt" from a man (including the possibility of painful disease and even death) is not as significant as the "hurt" to be incurred from women.

All three women are illustrative of my understanding of the deficits in the early mother/daughter relationship, conceptualized by me in the form of the introjection process—in these cases a disruptive one. The fact that all three teach brings home to me their attempts to master what I believe to be some very traumatic underpinnings in that process. What they did not "learn" from mother, they appear to be trying to "take in" in other ways. Teaching may provide that opportunity, albeit a limited one.

I would like to turn to a fourth and final illustration of a patient with whom I have been working analytically for three and an half years. I would like to use some poetic license (for how could analysts work if they could not?) and demonstrate what I believe to be an example of the parallel process at work as I struggled to understand and appreciate this idea of an encapsulated introject. Winnicott's own clinical work became more and more linked with the idea of communication in the potential space (Davis & Wallbridge, 1981, p. 65). "Psychotherapy," he said, "is done in the overlap of the two play areas, that of the patient and that of the therapist. If the therapist cannot play, then he is not suitable for the work. If the patient cannot play, then something needs to be done to enable the patient to become able to play, after which psychotherapy may begin" (Davis & Wallbridge, 1981, p. 65).

Missy

The patient, Missy, is a 28-year-old single woman who was referred to me by a female colleague because she "wanted to see a woman." She had been in treatment for several months with Dr. S, a male therapist by whom she had felt "intimidated." He had, she said, repeatedly asked her about sexual feelings for him, which left her feeling anxious and uncomfortable. She decided to leave treatment, whereupon he called her on the phone, threatened to bill for sessions missed and, ultimately, to take her to court for nonpayment. For Missy this was a reenactment of an earlier traumatic scene from childhood.

Missy is the youngest of four children. Her father was a brutal, violent man who drank and abused his wife and four children. Missy was abused physically and sexually, and felt as though both parents used her in their own private war with each other. By the time she was born, the marriage had deteriorated drastically, and mother often told her she was the reason for this.

Mother is a Jehovah's Witness who frowns upon "frivolity," which includes parties, makeup, or anything of a "sexual" nature. She frequently told her young daughter about father's "infidelities," which included sex with "black women and devils." She is a reclusive woman who keeps the house dark and wears dark glasses indoors. The parents were divorced when Missy was eight years old, and over time the older children (two girls and a boy), went to live with father, who had remarried. Missy was left to "care for mother" and "forced" to visit father on weekends. This, she says, caused her great anxiety. She was "afraid of him," and also "afraid" that mother would die or hurt herself, which she often threatened to do.

This arrangement lasted until Missy (in a move that I still deem to be somewhat miraculous) went away to college. She had managed to work after high school to finance this herself. She had had a tumultuous adolescence, replete with drugs and alcohol, but a long-term relationship with a boy throughout high school had been a somewhat stabilizing force in her life. (This young man very much represented the wished-for mother who would take care of her and protect her; something her mother was never able to do.) The relationship ended while she was away at school, which she called the most "devastating" time of her life. When she entered treatment with a man, she said it was to "kill two birds with one stone." She would work out her anger toward men and "somehow" manage to be less frightened by them.

What Missy experienced with Dr. S, she had experienced earlier with father. There was a feeling of being "sexually invaded," and she was left feeling enraged but, most of all, helpless. She turned to a woman (me) to "protect" her, as she had wished mother to do. She also has tremendous rage toward this mother/me, who not only failed to do this, but "pushed" her toward father long before she was ready to deal with the overwhelming feelings she had been prematurely exposed to.

At a time in treatment, when I was attempting to conceptualize what I have discussed here in terms of the encapsulated maternal introject, Missy was struggling to separate from mother and very much in the throes of guilt and anger at this woman about whom she is so ambivalent. She had moved out of mother's house and in with a young woman who, not surprisingly, had many of mother's characteristics. She had just bought new furniture, something she felt mixed about since she was, in effect, "getting rid" of mother's old stuff (which she had been using) in the process. She was also preparing for a trip to Ireland to visit a sister, a trip she was also conflicted about. She knew I had been to Ireland the summer before, so there was identification. She was traveling with her brother, however, so there were all kinds of incestuous ramifications, as well as the feelings about leaving me/mother for such a long separation. She reported this dream shortly before the trip:

> I had been scraping my toenails before I went to sleep. I have this dry skin, a kind of fungus thing. This is what I dreamt:
>
> I had this ingrown toenail. In the dream, I was picking at it. This black, slimy thing came out of my toe. I went to put it in the sink, but it kept sticking to me. I tried to get it off. Finally, I got it down the drain. My toe was bleeding but it felt OK. The pressure was off and it didn't hurt.
>
> At the end of the dream,, I was asking someone what to do.

She associated to "two things that I think of immediately." One was to "here and talking," "getting things out." The other was to the furniture, "getting rid of mother's things." Then she added, "It was like 'in a case,' 'clear,' 'a sac.'" She illustrated with her hands how big it was (she cupped her two hands).

There were associations to bleeding, menses, mother and fungus, and contamination. What is pertinent for purposes of this writing is her description of the "sac." I had been thinking along the lines of a small capsule at first, rather like a cold capsule. My own associations had led me to the idea of a mussel, a sac-like softer version of a cold capsule, and somewhat larger. A mussel has a black border around its edge. I remember being in that state of "suspended attention" we analysts speak of, listening with my own psyche hard at work, yet relaxed in the process. I can remember thinking as well, "This is exactly what I have been thinking about in terms of the encapsulated introject theory!" For the patient, the dream obviously did not have the significance it had for me. She is working on issues related to separation, for one, and defending against a very eroticized transference (as are the other patients discussed. Being close to a woman means working through the homosexual feelings, which include the loving and the hating feelings).

When I mentioned "poetic license" before, I was referring to that creative process wherein we analysts "play" in a sense in our own unconscious in order to better understand the patient. Simply put, the patient used a symbol, the "black, slimy thing," to illustrate her own unconscious conflicts, and it "fit" with what I had been contemplating in terms of the encapsulated maternal introject.

I would like to comment on what I think is an interesting and pertinent observation regarding this last patient in contrast to the others. She shows evidence of much of the same concreteness they do. However, where they, by virtue of their very fragile defense systems are only able to tolerate once-weekly sessions at present, Missy is coming three times a week and contemplating a fourth session. She uses the couch and free associates beautifully. The others are not able to use the couch but prefer sitting up in order to "see" me, something they have all verbalized. Missy, who has particular dynamics that predispose her to the couch (namely, a wish to "hide"), nevertheless, in spite of what would appear to have been a much more traumatic childhood, is able to use the analytic process in a way the others are not. She began treatment with more fluid boundaries and tremendous acting out compared to the others. (Her acting out takes more benign forms now.) I have wondered about genetic endowment as well as her ability to "take" from the environment what she needs (which may still have genetic underpinnings). It is also interesting to speculate as to what may have occurred in the earlier mother/child relationship that allowed her, in a sense, to grow. Was there some of Winnicott's "female element potential" in mother? To what extent did Missy (with mother's "permission") preserve a part of herself to care for mother? We could say that part of their "unspoken" agreement was that Missy would retain some part of herself (not accessible to mother) in order to care for mother, which had always been her role. Missy, on the other hand, needed her own "space," safe from mother, where she could have freedom from some of the overwhelming feelings that often threatened to overtake her.

Missy was able to play and reports having had an imaginary friend as a child. Her "friend" served many purposes for her. She also has the ability to symbolize and appears to have been able to create a "space" for herself sometimes when she needed to. My sense is that the other patients discussed were not able to do this. They are just learning to "play" in the analytic setting.

Whether the analyst takes the role of the "unobtrusive analyst" à la Balint, or allows or helps create Winnicott's "holding environment," the heart of the matter, as I see it, is that he or she must be able to use that facility that is involved in the capacity to play. (In an unpublished paper on working with children, I commented on the ability to move back and forth between primary and secondary process thinking as a prerequisite for working with children, as the analyst is required to both "play" as the child "directs," and "observe and interpret" as necessary.)

Transference Considerations

I would like to refer briefly to Khan's (1974) paper on the "use" of the analyst in the clinical situation. He says, of one patient, that she had set herself and the analyst the "essential" task of rediscovering and resolving the internalized and dissociated relation to her mother, which she had hidden in a very special way. The emphasis in the transference was on "knowing," and "that freeing of both imagination and intellectual capacities which alone enables a person to cognize themselves meaningfully" (p. 217).

In the second example, he tells us, the role of the analyst was to "curtail interpretative work because it merely reinforced the patient's own style of self defense" (p. 218). He states further: "No true object-relation is involved in this use of the analyst by the patient. The analyst is a living and responsive part of the total environment that the patient has put himself in the care of" (p. 218).

In a third and final illustration, he says, "The crux of the clinical situation lies in finding ways of enabling a patient to tolerate the violent rejection of the analytic process and helping him discover how he defends against the exposure of his inner reality" (p. 218). The need and compulsion to be found out, he says, citing work from Winnicott and Milner, is akin to what Winnicott has described as "the element of hope in the antisocial tendency" and "must be met as such."

Reading this, I was struck by how each of the above examples, at a given time in the treatment, might apply to any one of the patients discussed. As Khan points out, what is not discussed often is what he calls the "fluctuating interplay in the patient's total experience of himself in the analytic setting in terms of 'being'; through the object-relationships provided via transference toward 'experiencing'; and the 'knowing' of his intrapsychic reality and interpersonal conflicts through interpretation" (pp. 204–205).

With my patients, one of the most significant transference issues has involved their concreteness, which translates to their inability to "let me in" psychically, for the reasons I have indicated. Like any symptom, this must be understood and respected. Because both loving and hating feelings, which I believe have been encapsulated through this introjection process, are experienced as overwhelming, erotic feelings toward me must be kept away to avoid the ego being overrun by them. Incidentally, this presents quite a task for the analyst in terms of often corresponding countertransference feelings, since generally we are discussing very early, primitive feeling states. Nevertheless, as my experience is demonstrating, the patients continue to come to sessions, and there is discernible movement. It remains for me to continue to understand what is happening with the patients, what is being experienced by me, and what is going on in what Khan refers to as the "fluctuating interplay" between us. Putting this paper together has been a way of understanding and experiencing as well.

Summary

I have tried to show how a disruptive early mother/child relationship may lead to what I have conceptualized as an "encapsulated maternal introject." Due to what would have been experienced as overwhelming feeling states if the introject were fully assimilated, patients were obliged to "split off" the more toxic (suffocating, intrusive) aspects of mother in order to survive.

My sense is that mother, due to her own deficits, was not able to tolerate even a gesture that she perceived as separate from her, leading her daughter to defensively encapsulate part mother while allowing the rest to be assimilated. The result, in the cases of patients I have discussed, is a "concreteness" which becomes evident early in treatment.

Comparing my concept to Giovacchini's "frozen introjects," I discussed some of the theoretical underpinnings of the introjection process.

The women discussed function well in their professional lives (taking their professional identity from fathers). They appear feminine in dress and mannerisms, yet have a difficult time in the area of female relationships, in particular.

One of my speculations is that mothers were not able to allow their daughters to "be" or "play" in a way that fosters separation and autonomy, and to this end, I used Winnicott's work on play and the "potential space" to illustrate and clarify the need for this.

My "understanding" of all of this came about as a result of my own "playing" in the unconscious area we analysts use to process patients' conscious and unconscious material. In a particular case, my "playing" dovetailed with the patient's symbolic representation in a dream dealing significantly with separation, and I used this as an example of parallel process.

Finally, I touched on some of the transference issues, including difficulties allowing me "in," which translates to the need to defend against both loving and hating feelings toward women.

References

Davis, M., & Wallbridge, D. (1981). *Boundary and space: An introduction to the work of D. W. Winnicott.* New York: Brunner/Mazel.

Deutsch, H. (1965). Some forms of emotional disturbance and their relationship to schizophrenia. In *Neuroses and character types* (pp. 262–281). New York: International Universities Press.

Ferenczi, S. (1909). Introjection and transference. In: *First contributions to psychoanalysis.* London: Hogarth Press, 1952.

Giovacchini, P. L. (1975). *Character disorders and adaptive mechanisms.* New York: Jason Aronson, 1984.

Kestenberg, J. S. (1957). Vicissitudes of female sexuality. In *Children and parents: Psychoanalytic studies in development.* New York: Jason Aronson.

Khan, M. M. R. (1974). Vicissitudes of being, knowing and experiencing in the therapeutic situation. *The privacy of the self: Papers on psychoanalytic theory and technique.* New York: International Universities Press.

Ogden, T. H. (1986). *The matrix of the mind: Object relations and the psychoanalytic dialogue.* Northvale, NJ: Jason Aronson.

Somatic Symptoms, Psychoanalytic Treatment, Emotional Growth

Ronald W. Levin, M.D.

The accepted technological approach to treatment of an eating disorder patient with psychophysiologic symptoms is a team approach to medical care, with each member of the team focusing on one aspect of the patient's illness (Hamburg et al., 1989). The medical and psychological treatment of such patients—usually women—can continue for years, with intermittent hospitalizations to control their symptoms and keep them out of physical or psychological danger (Herzog & Copeland, 1985; Hsu, 1986).

Case reports of psychoanalytic treatment of bulimic and anorectic women indicate that a technological treatment approach may contribute to the patient's complicated medical course (Mintz, 1985; Risen, 1982; Silverman, 1989). Technological medical care leads caretakers to conceptualize physical and behavioral symptoms as disease, while overlooking the level of emotional development of the patient; the unconscious meaning of the patient's words, actions, and somatic processes are also ignored (Lipowski, 1967). As a result, patients treated technologically often do not develop emotionally. Conflicts remain unresolved and actively contribute to symptoms (Lipowski, 1988).

In contrast, in a developmental approach, the unconscious meaning of the patient's actions and words are interpreted, thereby placing the focus of treatment on the emotional processes of the patient, not on control of symptoms (Hogan, 1985; Sperling, 1967;

Wilson, 1985). Such an approach results in treatment and outcome markedly different from those of a technological approach. The contrast in success of treatment and outcome may be mistakenly attributed to some difference in disease or personality strengths. This is not the case. Patients treated developmentally appear different because their psychological defenses and conflicts as well as their underlying painful reality are brought into focus by treatment (Sperling, 1973; Wilson, 1989). This not only provides the impetus to restart emotional growth, but also puts dramatic psychophysiologic symptoms in perspective, allowing the therapist to tolerate the patient's symptoms without resorting to technological intrusion and control (Giovacchini, 1975).

The four-year analytic treatment of a 22-year-old English woman named B, who had seizures and an eating disorder, illustrates the different course and outcome provided by a developmental viewpoint. Although the patient had one grand mal seizure during treatment, she was able to stop her antiseizure medication when she completed treatment and has been seizure-free for more than six years. More importantly, she matured with treatment and was able to control her symptoms, engage in stable relationships, and pursue her own goals. She could function on a more autonomous level.

B had intense behavioral and emotional symptoms that could have easily served as a rationale for medical or pharmacological intervention. Her history was typical of difficult eating disorder patients in that it included somatic symptoms and several caretakers. Therapy centered on individuation, although its achievement was solidified through sexual metaphor.

At the start of treatment, B was in crisis. She felt directionless and lost in her life and had been rejected by a previous therapist who "accidentally" kept locking her out of her office building. B used marijuana and amphetamines and forced herself to vomit up to four and five times daily. As a result, she missed work as a shop clerk frequently. She took Valium when available and drank five glasses of wine at night. B had daily petit mal seizures, which she described as staring, loss of alertness, head nodding, and tremulousness. The seizures began in latency and were diagnosed as petit mal in early adolescence. She also had had 10–20 grand mal seizures over the previous 10 years. They began in midadolescence.

Early in life, B was cared for by a succession of people, and her early memories were of feeling cheated. Her mother was chronically angry at her father, who was not responsive to her anger. When B was a teenager, her parents separated and divorced. She was left with her mother, who threatened to overdose in front of her. She tried to remain in contact with her father, who she felt ignored her. During this period, she began vomiting. In college, B developed a relationship with another student. When the relationship ended, she attempted suicide and was hospitalized.

When I first saw this patient, she was hesitant to speak, looked depressed and awkward, but said that what she wanted was a "good shrink." Nonetheless, her first year of treatment was characterized by ambivalence and confusion. She had intense emotional and physical reactions to any understanding I offered. Several times, she tried to break off treatment.

During her early appointments, B reported the week's events of parties and alcohol and drug use with intense urgency. When I asked about reasons for the intense feelings, she wept until her appointment was over. While she cried, she would talk about her epilepsy, stealing, absences from work, and abuse of drugs.

Just before her fifth appointment, B called to cancel her session but changed her mind when I asked what was up. At the beginning of her session, I asked if she was uncomfortable with treatment, and B told me that she wanted some control in her life. I told her that psychotherapy could perhaps bring her that control, and, later in the hour, she considered making firm arrangements for treatment.

Over the next couple of sessions, she felt as if she were in a fog and couldn't do anything for herself, while she talked about her mother's concerns about her father's situation. I said that she seemed burdened by her mother's reality and couldn't see her own.

In the next session, B made another commitment: a decision to begin twice-a-week treatment, which I had originally recommended. But she felt paranoid, giggled throughout the hour, and described herself as being guarded. She was concerned that a friend would find out what she was doing. I said that perhaps this was related to how she felt about treatment. B told me I was too young and that I would take things away from her.

In the following few sessions, she complained of loneliness and had depersonalized episodes, while her vomiting and drug abuse increased. She complained of feeling locked up and chaotic with no place to live. When she closed her eyes during one hour, she saw an old woman with purple coming out of her mouth, while she saw me as having a purple pillow in my mouth. I understood this as her view of relationships and, in my mind, connected her feelings of having no place to live with relationships that did not involve reciprocity or any sense of psychological holding.

During the tenth session of these intense symptoms, while complaining of not liking work, having no real home, and disliking her boss, she began to play with Kleenex and tied it into a knot. When I asked what she was doing, she looked at the Kleenex, spread it into a tie and remembered how her father looked. Then she put the Kleenex into her hair, tilted her head, and smiled like a little girl. I wondered out loud if she was remembering being a little girl who missed her father. With that she sobbed, but when she pulled herself together, she remembered her recent visit home. Her room had been redecorated and was now totally different from the time of her youth. She realized, with some depth, that she had really meant it when she said she had no home.

In the following hour, she decided that she wanted to live alone, requested a lower fee, reported feeling more competent, and told me about her inheritance. These did not fit together logically, but they were indications of increased psychological strength. She was beginning to individuate. She also told me that she was in a dangerous spot in psychotherapy and wanted to leave. She felt treatment was a big deal and was not going to be a replay of her previous therapy. It was private, intimate, personal. As we prepared for a vacation break, she had to interrupt her hour to move her car and felt everything was falling apart.

By the time I returned from vacation, B reported she had been drinking every night, wanted only to escape feelings, felt something was missing, and complained that things were going too fast. Her hours were spent crying, but she would also arrive early for appointments and after appointments would sit and cry in the stairwell near my office.

When she was late paying her bill, I asked about this, and B told me that she thought that I would let her be the way she was until she was ready to pull herself together. She missed her next appointment and then reported drinking and stealing. I asked if this was connected to my raising the issue of the bill. In response, B said that she would pay the bill every month, but at her next appointment she reported headaches, which she had never had before, made plans for a vacation, and cancelled them. She also reported spending a weekend alone for the first time during her treatment. Although her ambivalence was obvious, realistic limits had led to another increase in psychological strength.

B decided to go home in order to discuss partial financial support for treatment. She reported a dream whose contents she could not remember. Her associations were that she had found a bag of potatoes with maggots in it and had thrown it out without fully opening it. She went on to talk about the last time she had asked her mother for something and how intrusive her mother became. When B said she was worried about the garbage between her mother and her, I asked if she could remember her dream. She said the dream was about storage. She remembered maggots and then said that what she was storing was making her sick. This was an indication of strengthened psychological boundaries. She could store something and was aware of it.

When B began to complain of depression and painful feelings, I suggested that she consider psychoanalysis. She said she felt trapped, vulnerable, and intruded upon. She feared she would be lost in her own thoughts and hoped for a magical cure, but also felt excited about the prospect of more intensive treatment. B requested sleeping pills and had dreams of feeling violated at work. She came late to appointments, vomited, got sick, missed work, and was demoted. She hated herself. She remembered being rejected by her father and wanting to leave home, but she also remembered worrying about her mother's life, which had stopped her from leaving home. She increased her use of drugs. I didn't say much during this time, and she dreamt: I was there but when she turned around to look I had turned into a Ken doll. In her dream, because she had to turn around to look at me, it appeared she was already in psychoanalysis.

After five sessions, B blurted out that she felt safe only in my office. I wondered out loud what she was thinking about analysis. B said she couldn't make any decision and remembered the first few times that she was interested in a boyfriend. She would show little interest in him but hoped her boyfriend would show interest in her. She wanted me to make her commitment for her. When B realized this, she decided to begin psychoanalysis.

The therapeutic alliance was defined and consolidated during this first year of treatment. It was not an alliance designed to control symptoms, but an alliance designed to understand the emotional meanings of the patient's verbal and somatic expressions. Technological treatment of B's symptoms would not have led to this type of treatment relationship or focus because technological approaches divorce symptoms from their underlying meanings, leaving patients without effective emotional communication. Empathic interpretation of feelings and actions without control allowed the openness and intimacy that are necessary for emotional development.

During the first months of psychoanalysis, B had strong desires to know more about me, coupled with memories of sneaking into other families' houses to steal food. When she asked questions about me and expressed guilty feelings, I said she was trying to sneak into my house and felt guilty about it. This transference interpretation led to her having concerns about wanting too much, fears of getting too excited about things, and some sense that her vomiting and seizures were connected to this. "I do feel like exploding at times. I control it all the time. I got amphetamines to control my weight. It worked, but now I control things. I really want to explode, but I just put a lid on things. Maybe my vomiting has something to do with that."

As she began to connect control, exploding, vomiting, and seizures, B felt she was falling apart and had fevers over the weekends. She felt "seizurish" as she struggled with limits. She was caught owing $500 in parking fines; her mother had the telephone operator interrupt her phone calls; she had a sexual dream about relatives. All of these were connected to conflict about limits and lack of limits. She hated the end of therapy hours and asked to leave one session 10 minutes early. Although I felt some temptation to agree to her request, I did not.

In the next session, B reported a dream of a small ceremony in a wooded area. A big barge came up, and a man said they weren't supposed to be there. The man that she was with "jumped" that man, a military man killed him and his skin came off, which she described in detail and which she felt was "really gross." The dream seemed confused. Her associations were to feeling relieved when she was understood, but then feeling overwhelmed by how much she had to do.

I believed she felt that limits led to improvement but also to increased awareness of her confusion. I thought the increasing confusion in her dream was related to feeling overwhelmed. B also complained: "I used to seize after vomiting. I can't tell you; it's too uncomfortable; I'm too ashamed. I don't understand it; it's not under my control. I always have trouble with limits."

Over the next few sessions, B said she was "hedging" as she talked about work, where she was obtaining some recognition for improved performance. With some reluctance—she described it as putting a lid on things—she talked about vomiting, urges to explode, and needs for control. When she wondered why she continued to vomit even though she no longer ate with her mother, I said she still put a lid on things because she was afraid she'd take in too much, as she did with her mother. She spent the weekend ill, imagined seeing me behind her throughout the weekend, and wanted to move in with a girlfriend. I thought she believed she needed protection from me as well as from her own feelings.

B explained that when her vomiting started, her father had just left, and she was an adolescent alone with her mother. Her mother would stuff her with food, which she would have to eat to protect her mother from pain. She ate to fill her mother up. But then B added, "Somehow that doesn't explain it. The vomiting is over there, it's not really me. I don't want to own up to it. I have to treat it nicely. I couldn't get mad at my mother. She needed me so badly and was so sad. There was no way I could get mad at her. My mother couldn't let go."

B asked for a prescription for Valium from me. I told her that that was one way to deal with her feelings but questioned if it would help her understand them. She told me that the night before she had taken Valium, Dilantin, peanuts, and cheese and ended up vomiting. B went on to say that she hadn't vomited in three or four nights and felt as if she was giving up something. The next day she dreamt of stealing things and trying to undo the stealing by putting things back, but finding out that everything was nailed down. She felt disgusted in the dream because everything had been nailed down. As B explored her feelings of disgust she realized she always tried to steal but ended up stealing from herself. This led to memories of a relative who stole.

After she had been in psychoanalysis for five months, her mother visited, and they went on a whirlwind tour that left B confused, feeling weird, and not remembering what happened. She wondered if she had had a seizure. At the same time, she received a promotion at work. In her appointments she felt excited; she remembered past relationships and realized she had always had a boyfriend until she had started analytic treatment. It appeared to me that the transference relationship was consolidating. She was less symptomatic outside of therapy, but more stimulated by her relationship to me.

The next hour—the end of the analytic week—she felt anxious, confused, and worried about her promotion. She wanted to be comforted and complained of a headache. I said she felt the promotion was too much for her, just like she felt her mother was too much for her. The next day she had a grand mal seizure.

B was disappointed. She said everything was going too fast and she couldn't absorb it. In a dream she reported, she was in a parking garage with many levels and machines to take cars up. The earth was ruined, she was stuck on the earth part with her family, suddenly the ground fell through, and she couldn't get out. The dream indicated that B's hope for a mechanical solution for her problems was now irrelevant. She knew that would not get her out of her situation. She would have to work emotionally.

Over the weekend, B went to see her father. On the way there she felt anxious and couldn't relax. Then she thought about where she was going and what she was feeling. That realization calmed her down and made her feel better. It was also evidence of her ability to constructively identify with treatment.

Vomiting again became prominent while she dreamt and talked of being emotionally involved with me. "My contacts [lenses] have RL on them, your initials. I think about you in the bathroom. Your initials make me feel good. Every time I come into the bathroom I think of you, even when I'm throwing up. What a wonderful way to be close to you." She was now more comfortable with her emotions.

B missed an appointment because she overslept, called me in anguish, and received a second appointment for the same day. During the appointment, she became disorganized. In the next session, she reported a dream about getting two cars for the price of one, and telling the person in the dream, "You aren't in the business of selling cars." B also reported a dream in which she was a little girl who was in the way of a man and woman who were getting emotionally involved and who was ignored while vomiting. She was anxious about having two appointments in one day, criticized her lack of limits, and questioned if I was testing her by giving her the second appointment. I said she had asked for a second appointment because she was lonely and I gave her one because it was available, but to her it represented a loss of psychological boundary and made her anxious. B told me that treatment was the core of her day because she now worked at night and her appointment was the only activity of her day. "I'm scared to be that invested. You're my only ear. I have no reason to trust. It's not safe."

She thought of me as her sedative, wanted to marry me, and acted seductively. When B said she thought her mother felt it was all right to act seductively, I interpreted her wish to seduce me because that is what she felt her mother had done to her therapist to obtain comfort. She remembered how she always felt out of control and was never sure of what she could and could not do. She said she preferred to have seizures rather than feel bad and cry. It was not safe for B to trust because she never knew if she was being played with, being used, or being taken seriously. She also did not know if she was playing, using, or being serious.

After a visit to her mother, she said she felt like a nothing at home and like a person in treatment. At home her only purpose was to fill her mother's needs. "I'm very affectionate with my mother, too much this weekend, so I withdrew. I have a lot of feelings toward my mom, I guess. I'm so scared of those feelings, I can't stand it. I have them; I don't like them."

When B received a large raise in her salary, she decided to increase her appointments to five times weekly, but she had dreams of balloons being deflated and complained that the fifth hour cost too much and of feeling intimidated by her feelings for me. When B said she felt bad about the fifth hour, I said that she wanted the fifth hour but felt bad about having to pay for it. It was the limits that bothered her.

B dreamt that she was scared about getting married and went to her father who protected her by saying it was okay. She felt angry about how involved she was with me and told me that she was even scheduling her meals around analysis. She dreamt about escalators that went backwards, felt depersonalized, and in an attempt to make more money to pay for a fifth hour, applied for a new job. B dreamt about wanting to be committed but felt unsafe and was angry with me because she felt I wasn't listening to her. Finally she said that she needed to talk about the fee because she could not afford to pay for five appointments weekly at her present fee. A small reduction in the fee was made.

She wanted to bring me a gift. "I feel uncomfortable. I was going to bring you a gift, a plant that needed water every now and then, soaking, not just a little water. I feel I need more than I actually do . . . thinking of that time that I enjoyed sex, I didn't think of it as psychological. Now I'm wondering, feeling guilty. If I'm separate I can feel fulfilled. Any Joe on the street would be better sexually than someone I'm close to. I feel like I'm being absurd."

B had feelings of unattachment and remembered her mother being pushy. I said that she felt unattached because, even with a fee reduction, I couldn't make up for her feelings of lack of mothering. She thought of how she had to care for her mother. "I feel like half a person. When I talk it is scary. I feel like nothing. I'm there to fill a void. I relay messages. I filled my mother's needs, and she talked to my father through me. That's why I was born. When I do something for myself, it makes me sick." Her birth was a gift to her father to try to cement her parents' marriage; she had failed to do that and, therefore, felt valueless.

After this insight, there was a noticeable slowing in the pace of our interactions. She was able to talk about her feelings more openly, and there was increased comfort between us. Now, when her mother planned a visit, she was angry that her mother was visiting. She had a dream of saying no to free gifts and when asked to make accommodations for her mother with a friend, B told her that it would be more appropriate for her to make her own arrangements.

When I announced a vacation, B immediately planned one of her own. When she realized she was reacting to her feelings about my leaving, she decided she could tolerate them. In her hours she felt lonely and disoriented. She feared that her feelings would be cut off by my plans for her and that I wouldn't let her feelings evolve without leaving. "I'm too depressed to talk about how I feel. I'm afraid you don't feel I'm making progress. I'm so lonely it's scary, I don't even know what I'm feeling. I'm afraid if I talk about my bad feelings, my angry feelings, that I'll be too frail to handle them. I'll get in and not be able to get out." I told her treatment would continue until she felt she had dealt with her problems, and she once again became involved.

For the first time during treatment, she became involved with a man. As B became more interested in him, she felt anxious at being "unplugged" from me and feared I would disapprove of their relationship. She talked more about her boyfriend and seemed to ignore her problems. When their relationship became the focus of her hours and she continued to tell me how wonderful she felt, I told her that her relationship with her boyfriend was one thing, but her analysis to deal with her problems was another. This led to angry feelings toward me, and at the end of the week she spoke of her powerful, sexual feelings and her fears of my powerful, sexual feelings. B now understood at an emotional level that we were two separate individuals.

As the time of my vacation arrived, B felt sad and dreamt of taking her own trip and of being in my office with my wife who had pretty dresses. She was jealous of my wife, worried about me, and aggravated with her boyfriend. I said that she was worried about her aggravation with me, but she told me she thought I was going where her father's old girlfriend had become ill. While I was gone, she looked up my name in a medical directory, typed out all the data she could find about me, framed it, and put it on her desk.

B's mother became reluctant to continue her partial financial support of the psychoanalysis, and B again asked for a fee reduction. She was concerned that her mother would destroy the analysis. I told her that her analysis was real and if the fee had to be lowered in order to continue her treatment I would consider that. In response, she became disorganized, felt suicidal, and began to question if lowering the fee would be good for her. She decided instead to talk to her mother about the importance of her treatment. It appeared to me that B had accepted the importance of limits.

B ended her relationship with her boyfriend, who she felt was too passive for her. "I feel better, well taken care of. I want you to attend to me more. There is an urgency to it. This is the only part of the day that counts and everything centers around it. But I have a new feeling; I can really feel you behind me. I feel it emotionally. My father didn't attend to me and I wanted him to." With limits consolidated, she could allow herself to be closer to others. Her relationships were not only safer, but also more fulfilling.

She wanted to wear more feminine dresses, and began to recognize other people who she thought affected our relationship. B became afraid that she was too independent and that I wouldn't give her what she needed because of that independence. She was afraid I wouldn't like her because of that. But when B thought she saw another patient in the bathroom before her hour, she said, "She doesn't know I see you; she looked blank. I felt uncomfortable, I wanted to get in her way, move her aside; I felt like pushing her."

B had dreams of the two of us in a pool holding little frogs and smoking them and of being on a towline which she couldn't get off. "I realize I'll never get anything out of you. I can't stand it. All I ever do is pull stuff out of you. All you do is not give it to me. A lot of fun and I pay for it."

Her focus turned to work and her interest in taking over her supervisor's position. She dreamt of being at a beach and having her co-workers insist that she return to work; then she dreamt of her mother saying they were of the same gender and telling her she had close relationships with women. I told her that while she wanted increased responsibility at work she was afraid of ending up in a regressive relationship with her mother.

My vacation led to some disorganization. B felt lonely and depressed. She cried while I was away, and she gained five pounds. At the end of my vacation she attempted to call me. Upon my return, she dreamt of a man who was castrated and a woman who was going to be punished. She said she felt like leaving and that she was angry at me.

Her treatment was interrupted by a medical problem that her internist wanted evaluated. When she returned to treatment after a short absence, she dreamt of a woman who wanted so much that she was bloated and required a needle to release the contents. She thought of what was inside of her and how in the past she had taken in anything. Then she realized that if she really wanted something before she took it in, she wouldn't have to throw up.

B wanted to show off her connection to me by coming to her appointment one or two minutes late, which would enable her to walk into my office in front of other patients in the waiting room. She dreamt about me and imagined that I was watching while she talked to other men. I said she felt left out in her relationship to me because of my outside life and wanted me to feel as left out as she felt. She told me how involved she was, how she felt competitive with my wife and wanted me to obtain a divorce, and how people now gave her more space and listened to what she said. B was feeling stronger. She became involved with a man who was less maternal than the other men she had dated. She talked of knocking over a vase of mine because it got in her way and connected this to her feelings about my wife.

As her sexual and aggressive feelings increased, she began to have fears that she would be closed out. "I'm so involved, probably too involved, and want to leave, but you are holding me together." She dreamt something about a baby, thought overtly about having babies and then of her analysis possibly coming to an end. She became panic stricken because she was afraid of being disconnected from me; she dreamt of going to the dry cleaners and making a big mistake in front of other people. I said she was more independent but feared she had been taken to the cleaners. She said she had changed and that she could now be separate from me but still remain connected to me. She dreamt of disgusting things and talked about her relationship to her boyfriend. I said she was afraid I would find her relationship disgusting.

B dreamt of me teaching a class concerning $2 \times 2 + 2$ but she couldn't get the problem. She also dreamt of being given a test by her grandmother, in which she had to marry a man who was assertive. She remembered how all the men in her family were passive and how her mother and her mother's mother dominated everyone. I said she was afraid she wouldn't get her mother's approval if she married an assertive man. She felt sexual and worried that she was going off on the wrong track. I said she hoped that I would stop her because she was afraid I would disapprove of her sexual feelings. Earlier, any man would do; now she wanted to marry a man with particular traits. The person had become important to her. This allowed her to perceive the passivity in the men of her family. Her mother's disapproval of emotionally mature men had become apparent to her.

As the holidays approached, the mood of her dreams and presentation changed. B became lonely. She felt challenged by something and wondered if I was there. When I said she was competing for attention with my family because the holidays were approaching, B's symptoms changed.

Her eating and vomiting increased, and she began taking sleeping pills again. She felt sexual and told me that after work each night she would go to eat in a restaurant near my office and then return to her home to vomit. When B told me about her mother, who never understood her, I said she was looking for maternal care and attempting to get it through sex. During the next week, she complained of feeling feverish and having weak knees at work, but her vomiting stopped.

Over the next few weeks, she became more aware of a desire to have a baby. She dreamt of men throwing darts at a picture and thought of giving me a picture of herself, of darts in women's clothing to make room for breasts, and of puncturing. I said that made me think of penetration. She thought of my always getting a bull's eye, her periods, and her father's being alone. I said she wished to have my baby as she wanted to have her father's baby. She said no, she wanted to be her father's baby, but wanted to have my baby.

B became preoccupied with ending treatment. "I feel bad, real bad. I'm ahead of myself. Why? I'm in a race. I want to finish so others can't talk about finishing before I do." She dreamt of skiing off a mountain and said, "I'm afraid, because I'm feeling well, that you aren't as concerned."

Wishes for a more intimate relationship with me continued. "Still, I want to find out about you. I want to shake you up. I want to feel you." I said that if she knew about me, she felt she wouldn't have to deal with feelings about leaving me. She became sad and wondered what was important to her. "I've been thinking about my dad lately. How I write him off when actually he is very important to me. I think I really make an impression on him, but I'm not like him. I feel toward him like I do toward you, but I don't talk much about that in here."

B thought again about leaving and felt aggravated because she didn't know where she was going. She began vomiting again and dreamt of a door being closed. She felt lousy, while acknowledging that, in general, she felt much better.

She had a dream of having trouble graduating and said, "I feel unsteady, afraid I'll lose what I've got. I'd be afraid to drive by your office. Would my vomiting start again? I would miss you. I know you'll miss me, but it will hurt no matter what." When B decided that I could not forget her, she was able to set a date for termination.

The next day, B woke up crying, took a tranquilizer, and didn't want to come to her appointment. She dreamt of a labor relations lawyer leaving. It was a great big deal. She said, "When I feel good I'm afraid it isn't real. I want someone to lean on. What will happen when I get into trouble? If I can't get things figured out, I'll come and see you." She thought about exceptions and overtime, which I said were connected to wishes to return after she finished. Then she wanted to quit analysis rather than deal with the feelings she was having and finally decided that the whole thing was for nothing.

B dreamt about coming to see me, parking on the first level, and seeing that after the fourth level the coding changed in the elevator. She said she had been in treatment four years and that maybe leaving was more than she could do. Her drinking increased as she talked about feeling empty and more alone. "I don't want to be with all this horrible stuff. I don't want to leave feeling brave; I want to leave feeling good."

I asked if she was really comfortable with termination. She said, "I can't hardly stand it. I'm anxious, that's how comfortable I am. No matter how I leave, I'll be thinking I could have left better. Somewhere you have to draw the line. I can come back. It's not the end of the world, but it makes a difference in how I live. I'm in the refinement section. If I need to stay here I'll do it. I'll go when I'm ready. I think you underestimate me."

Over the next week, she became sad and cried a lot: "All of me has changed, parts of me have changed, but what I'll miss is you. You seem less and less important, which makes it easier for me, but you've been right on."

In our last appointment, B reported a dream: "I was in a restaurant. There were two or three of us. Somebody got something that wasn't good. I told them to take it back. We got other things and got milk shakes on top of it." She said, "I'll miss this place. I feel good."

B came back one month later when she had a dream she interpreted as a suicidal wish. She said, "I wish you would take me back in a different way. I feel uncomfortable. My supervisor said I made an error in judgment. I said I didn't, but acknowledged she was the boss. That's when I started my own business. We'll see what happens."

Three months later, B returned again and had dreamt of my being concerned she'd be caught in a storm and of coming to my office where she got an electric charge. She said, "I haven't been getting the attention I want. The way things are going in my life now, I like it and I don't like it. Maybe that is a fact of life. I'm way below therapeutic level on my medicine now. I told my mother I had to get off the phone because I was in a hurry to go out with my dad. She was taken aback. I'll see what happens."

This was a process of individuation. During treatment, B evolved from chaos to more organized symptoms. The treatment mobilized developmental processes. As emotional development restarted, intense feeling associated with primitive fantasy and action, as well as altered physiology, appeared. B was attempting to reenact the relationships experienced in her youth when she was cared for physically but not psychologically.

B's behavior was an invitation to control out-of-control impulses. But direct attempts to control without understanding would have limited development because, early in treatment, her developmental changes did not fit together logically. They appeared chaotic, but these changes were evidence of increased ego strength. They were associated with increased trust and a more structured and organized relationship to another individual. In treatment, the patient was letting another person become important to her. This allowed her to become more aware both psychologically and physically of her own discomfort. She was identifying with the therapist's orientation of understanding emotion rather than reacting to it.

The recommendation for psychoanalysis was based on B's increased ability to feel, tolerate, and express her own emotions. Although these were primarily painful experiences, this, also, was a sign of developmental progress. Her reaction to my recommendation was intense. But the exacerbation of B's somatic and emotional symptoms required empathic responses and monitoring for danger—not control.

At the start of her psychoanalysis, after one year of psychotherapy, B was graphic in describing the options available to her to deal with stimulation and emotions. She could either put a lid on or explode. These represented her childhood perceptions of reactions to emotions in her family as well as her current repertoire of psychological defenses. Instead of reproducing her family defenses, her use of these defenses was interpreted. This led to intense reactions as the sense of intimacy in treatment increased. Because she had poor psychological boundaries, intimacy was associated with intrusion, which included both being intruded upon and intruding. This contributed to poor somatic and emotional function (Taylor, 1987).

As the therapy relationship consolidated around transference feelings and B's emotional life became increasingly organized around treatment, her psychological boundaries became more defined. This new organization made B anxious. She was afraid that intense emotions combined with limits would destroy treatment. Experience with her parents—who had responded to her as if she were an adult rather than an individuating child—made limits a punishing experience for her. This had led to her use of disavowal in responding to her own emotions and symptoms. B feared that I, too, would respond to her without any understanding of her level of psychological function. Her requests for medication were related to this fear. They expressed a wish to control and cover up confusion as well as to undo its effects.

As she developed emotionally, B became increasingly aware of her feelings and their sources. She used this knowledge to further her understanding of herself and other important figures in her life. This brought changes in her perceptions and changes in her psychological fears, as illustrated by her evolving reactions to me and her mother and father.

Early in her treatment, she was frightened by her reactions to the increasing intimacy of our relationship; later, she understood me as a part of her body which she could use for soothing; and, finally, she understood me as someone separate from her. At this time, she also realized she had a life of her own.

The same evolution occurred with her parents. At first, she not only feared psychological merger with her mother, but enacted it. Later in treatment, she could say no to her mother's requests, and, instead of reproducing a primitive symbiotic relationship, she began to fear the regressive aspects of her relationship with her mother. This involved a sense of separateness. Similarly, her relationship with her father evolved from one in which she feared being ignored to one in which she could exchange honest feelings.

B's seizures appear to have been psychological phenomena, although control of alcohol and drug use would affect an organic process by decreasing tendencies to seize. The seizures are probably best understood psychologically as dissociative and regressive episodes. As illustrated by her dream of the earth being ruined, the symbiotic foundation of B's psychological functioning had been ruined. To attempt to maintain ties to an experience with nurturing feelings, she regressed. The "seizure" was an attempt to reproduce an intimate, primitive relationship without psychological boundary.

She enacted this reproduction because she had little capacity to express sexual or aggressive striving or conflict constructively because of poor individuation. Her somatic reaction to feelings of intimacy early in treatment were examples of this. Mental mechanisms to control and express angry and sexual urges were inadequate, as were psychological boundaries separating her from others. Direct expression of these urges in this psychological setting was felt to be dangerous by B.

This changed in treatment. Her sexual and angry feelings became more adult as her defenses of externalization and projection were interpreted and her feelings—now more exposed—were shaped by reality. This allowed more psychological separation. She recognized this growing independence, but also feared other's reactions as she focused aggressive and sexual feelings toward them. Her feelings became more specific as she related them to people who had emotional meaning for her. She could feel sexual about me, jealous about my interactions with others, sad about our separations, and angry at those who she felt interfered with her.

Two areas of developmental pathology were present in B: Conflicts and emotions related to the omnipotent feeling of oneness with mothering figures, and conflicts and emotions related to mature angry and sexual feeling. The predominant feeling in the first was grief; the predominant feeling in the second was anxiety. Treatment was complicated by interaction between these two areas.

This interaction may occur more frequently in women because of the specific developmental issues women face in individuating. Mothers more easily identify with a baby of their own sex, making it more difficult to respond to differences related to natural endowments or phases of emotional development. The sense of loss with individuation is associated with narcissistic injury, which must be dealt with before higher level conflicts can be resolved (Clower, 1988).

B's mother would overwhelm her through stimulating interactions such as attempts to overdose or shopping sprees. She did not allow B to be different from her, and based on B's experience with feeding, appears to have valued submission. Without any ability to express herself individually, B could only regress at times of sexual or aggressive stimulation. This satisfied her mother's need for submission and reestablished a symbiotic union for B and her mother (Sperling, 1973).

B's regressive psychological attachment to others complicated her expression of anger and sexuality. But when she came to terms with realistic limits in relationships, she had to face loss. She also had to face the anxiety associated with internal conflict because her sexual and aggressive feelings were confusing to her and were rejected by her. She saw them as disgusting and feared the actions of others in retaliation.

Treatment of B required not only recognizing her level of emotional expression, but also recognizing the shifts in these levels and their changing defensive use to obscure feelings and different developmental conflicts. Treatment also required recognition of beginning individuation, which was associated with behavioral and emotional changes that appeared illogical. Failure to recognize the confusing changes of individuation occurring early in treatment may contribute to endless medical care in some eating disorder patients. Technological and didactic approaches to treatment, with their emphasis on normal behavior, are not associated with the individual understanding of behavior and feelings required for emotional growth.

In treatment, B's psychological capacity increased. Although she had an intense transference in which she experienced me as part of her body, she could dream and talk about her experiences. She began to understand her "seizures" as a substitute for feeling and could see that she was used as an extension of her mother to communicate to her father. These insights led to changes in behavior. She could be angry, she could say no, she could feel sexual. Her symptoms became less and less significant.

Far from requiring chronic medical care, B had developed emotionally and escaped the restrictions of the technological model of disease and medical treatment.

References

Clower, V. (1988). The acquisition of mature femininity. In *New views on gender.* Washington, DC: American Psychiatric Press.

Giovacchini, P. (1975). The ego and the psychosomatic state. In *Psychoanalysis of character disorders* (pp. 388–401). New York: Jason Aronson.

Hamburg, P., Herzog, D., Brotman, A., & Stasior, J. (1989). The treatment-resistant eating-disordered patient. *Psychiatric Annals, 19,* 494–499.

Herzog, D., & Copeland, P. (1985). Eating disorders. *New England Journal of Medicine, 313,* 295–303.

Hogan, C. C. (1985). Psychodynamics: Object relations. In C. P. Wilson (Ed.), *Fear of being fat: The treatment of anorexia nervosa and bulimia* (pp. 115–152). Northvale, NJ: Jason Aronson.

Hsu, L. K. G. (1986). The treatment of anorexia nervosa. *American Journal of Psychiatry, 143,* 573–581.

Lipowski, Z. J. (1967). Review of consultation psychiatry and psychosomatic medicine. *Psychosomatic Medicine, 29,* 201–224.

Lipowski, Z. J. (1988). Somatization: The concept and its clinical application. *American Journal of Psychiatry, 145,* 1358–1368.

Mintz, I. (1985). Psychoanalytic therapy of severe anorexia: The case of Jeannette. In C. P. Wilson (Ed.), *Fear of being fat: The treatment of anorexia nervosa and bulimia* (pp. 217–244). Northvale, NJ: Jason Aronson.

Risen, S. (1982). The psychoanalytic treatment of an adolescent with anorexia nervosa. *The Psychoanalytic Study of the Child, 37,* 433–460.

Silverman, M. (1989). Power, control and the threat to die in a case of asthma and anorexia. In C. P. Wilson & I. Mintz (Eds.), *Psychosomatic symptoms: psychodynamic treatment of the underlying personality disorder* (pp. 351–364). Northvale, NJ: Jason Aronson.

Sperling, M. (1967). Transference neurosis in patients with psychosomatic disorders. *Psychoanalytic Quarterly, 36,* 342–355.

Sperling, M. (1973). Conversion hysteria and conversion symptoms: A review of classification and concepts. *Journal of the American Psychoanalytic Association, 21,* 745–771.

Taylor, G. J. (1987). A revised view of the mother-infant relationship. In *Psychosomatic medicine and contemporary psychoanalysis* (pp. 117–142). Madison, CT: International Universities Press.

Wilson, C. P. (1985). The family psychological profile and its therapeutic implications. In *Fear of being fat: The treatment of anorexia nervosa and bulimia* (pp. 29–50). Northvale, NJ: Jason Aronson.

Wilson, C. P. (1989). Ego functioning in psychosomatic disorders. In *Psychosomatic symptoms: Psychodynamic treatment of the underlying personality disorder* (pp. 13–32). Northvale, NJ: Jason Aronson.

Daddy's Girl: An Interactional Perspective on the Transference of Defense in the Psychoanalysis of a Case of Father-Daughter Incest

Kenneth R. King, M.D., and
Theodore L. Dorpat, M.D.

> Daddy's girl
> In quiet desperation
> Sought dissociation
> From painful violation
> Bid heart and soul good-bye.
>
> Mrs. D, from "Daddy's Girl"

These lines just quoted from a poem by Mrs. D, whose analysis we shall describe, capture the sense of "deadening down" or "numbing out" that is so frequently part of the aftermath of incest.* Midway through her analysis, Mrs. D described herself as a "mechanical doll" who did not know who she was or what she felt; she had indeed bade her "heart and soul good-bye."

Although there is considerable psychiatric, epidemiologic, and case work literature regarding the incidence of, psychopathologic

* To preserve confidentiality, the patient's real name will not be used, and other identifying details will not be revealed.

effects of, and family characteristics surrounding sexual abuse and incest (Finkelhor, 1979; Goodwin et al., 1981; Herman, 1981; Mrazek & Kempe, 1981; Westen et al., 1990; Woodbury & Schwartz, 1971), there is still a meager literature with respect to psychoanalytic psychotherapy (Margolis, 1977, 1984; Stone, 1989b) and psychoanalytic group therapy (Ganzarain & Buchele, 1989) of incest victims. There is a mere smattering of psychoanalytic case reports regarding sexual abuse and seduction (Furman, 1956; Gillman, 1986; Katan, 1973; van Leeuwen, 1988; Williams, 1987) or incest per se (Abraham, 1907; Bernstein, 1989; Bonaparte, 1953; Dewald, 1989; Kramer, 1983; Levine, 1990; Rascovsky & Rascovsky, 1949; Reich, 1932; Richards, 1988; Shengold, 1980, Soll, 1984).

This is somewhat surprising, considering that Freud's (Breuer & Freud, 1895) original theory of pathogenesis was the famous seduction theory. Furthermore, even though Freud later (1914) shifted his focus to the complemental series, namely, the interplay of actual events and trauma, intrapsychic fantasy and conflict, and constitutional factors, to the end of his life he continued to stress the pathogenic importance of childhood seduction and sexual overstimulation (1917, 1918, 1933). Furthermore, Ferenczi (1933), one of the major psychoanalytic pioneers, described with penetrating insight in his last published paper the deep regressions and intense transference-countertransference reactions that occur in the analyses of incest victims. Perhaps because of the rift between Freud and Ferenczi at the time, this astounding paper, now considered by some to be a "rediscovered classic," which constitutes a pioneering application of object relations theory to the clinical situation, was ignored until recently (Rachman, 1989; Zaslow, 1988).

One of us (Dorpat, 1989) has hypothesized that for many years analysts, perhaps under the sway of an undue emphasis upon intrapsychic fantasy alone rather than its interdigitation with real life events, have unconsciously colluded with society's denial of incest. Thus, patients' previously repressed incest memories have often been treated as fantasies. Another possible explanation for the relative dearth of psychoanalytic case reports of incest is that many incest victims suffer such severe ego and characterologic disturbances that they are not suitable for psychoanalysis. Steele and Alexander (1981) report that incest victims often suffer from profound feelings of shame, guilt, and inferiority, along with "non-integrated identity, poor basic trust, repressed anger, unresolved identifications and fixations, and profound difficulties in establishing and maintaining warm, successful adult human relationships" (p. 233). Sexual dysfunctions and aberrations are a common residue of incest. Flugel (1953) found that nearly 70% of Chicago prostitutes were introduced to sex through father-daughter incest.

There is a growing body of evidence that severe sexual abuse, particularly incest, is commonly encountered in the history of patients with borderline personality disorders (Briere & Zaidi, 1989; Bryer et al., 1987; Gross et al., 1980–81; Herman, 1986; Herman et al., 1988; Ogata et al., 1990; Stone, 1981, 1989a, 1989b; van der Kolk, 1989; Westen et al., 1990; Zanarini et al., 1989; Zivney et al., 1988). There is a much higher frequency of an incest history among psychiatric patients than in the population as a whole, especially for hospitalized borderline, schizoaffective, and/or actively suicidal female patients (Stone, 1989a), and participants in patient-therapist sexual exploitation (Kluft, 1989). Suicide attempts are a particularly common clinical problem for incest victims (Brooks, 1982; Herman, 1986; Molnar & Cameron, 1975). A large percentage of patients with severe dissociative symptoms have suffered incest (Braun, 1984; Chu & Dill, 1990). Simpson and Porter (1981) find a significant link between self-mutilation in adolescent girls and earlier incestuous experiences. Richards (1988) reports a psychoanalytic case of father-daughter incest in which the patient engaged in self-mutilative acts. During psychoanalytic treatment, the dramatic recovery of the memory of intercourse with her father during late adolescence, along with memories and reconstructions of other sexual experiences with her father, proved central to the understanding of her self-mutilative behavior and her eventual cure.

Now psychoanalysts are "rediscovering" incest. In 1981 Anna Freud stated, "Far from existing only as a phantasy, incest is thus also a fact, more widespread among the population in certain periods than in others. Where the chances of harming a child's normal developmental growth are concerned, it ranks higher than abandonment, neglect, physical maltreatment or any other form of abuse. It would be a fatal mistake to underrate either the importance or the frequency of its actual occurrence" (p. 34). For the last few years there have been discussion groups at meetings of the American Psychoanalytic Association addressing the problem of sexual abuse and incest. Many of the recent case reports, however, are of child analytic patients who were sexually abused on a few occasions by people outside the immediate family and did not endure years of incest (Gillman, 1986; van Leeuwen, 1988).

Certainly sexual abuse and incest are prevalent problems. Furman and Furman (1984b) report that 10% of children who receive treatment at the Cleveland Child Analytic Clinic have been sexually abused and that the percentage is far greater in the private practices of Cleveland child analysts. The most recent epidemiologic study (Russell, 1986) revealed that 19% of San Francisco women have incurred incest, 4.5% with a father, adoptive father, or step-father. The actual figures are probably much higher, because women who are repressing or denying the trauma cannot be expected to answer such surveys accurately.

Our main intention in presenting aspects of the analysis of Mrs. D is to describe certain defenses that created difficulty in the transference-countertransference interplay and how careful analysis of these defenses and unconscious role relationships led not only to the revelation of past long-standing incest but also to characterologic change. (Here we are using countertransference in the broad sense of the term to include not only the analyst's own neurotic response to the patient, but also his reactions evoked by the patient's behavior toward him.) Incest patients may have intense transferences to the analyst or therapist who, in turn, may experience intense countertransference reactions. Some seasoned psychoanalytic veterans in this field (Ganzarain & Buchele, 1989) have advocated psychoanalytic group therapy using cotherapists, partially so that the transference-countertransference intensity can be kept at a manageable level. Countertransference reactions range from the therapist's wish to avoid or deny the horror of what has befallen the patient to a counterphobic or voyeuristic desire to "get all the details." Equally common is the therapist's avoidance of feeling guilty by opting to provide a "corrective emotional experience" by maintaining a nurturing role, rather than tolerating and interpreting the patient's negative transference and concomitant angry attacks upon the therapist. As Erna Furman (1989) has so wisely put it, the analyst "becomes the abuser and the abused." Difficulty tolerating being perceived as abusive contributes to many therapists focusing the patient upon "blaming the perpetrator" in the past. These strong transference-countertransference reactions tend to lead even experienced psychotherapists to focus predominantly upon the "there and then," namely, the details of the incest trauma, rather than the "here and now" resistances, transference, and interaction.

This is quite reminiscent of Breuer and Freud's (1895) long-outmoded abreaction model of therapy. The therapist's hot pursuit for memories of the incest experience can be an unconscious collusion on the therapist's part in repeating interpersonal aspects of the incestuous relationship. Though such an approach may have temporary palliative benefits, the inappropriate focus upon genetic and traumatic antecedents often interferes with the patient's changing the compulsive repetition in the present of prior destructive relationships. On the other hand, careful attention to resistances and interpretation of the patient's internalized object relations as they are subtly revealed, often nonverbally, in the therapeutic interaction may assist the therapist in avoiding enacting with the patient one more edition of a coercive and abusive relationship and help the patient see his or her active role in unconsciously eliciting such behavior.

Anna Freud (1936) decisively expanded the concept of transference when she described how the patient transfers into the analytic relationship not just impulses or wishes from the past but also characteristic defenses against such urges and their associated affects. This phenomenon she labeled transference of defense. Contemporary object relations theorists (Kernberg, 1976; Sandler, 1976a, 1976b; Sandler & Sandler, 1978) have further deepened the concept of transference to include how the patient may tend to repeat or "actualize" his or her self-and-object role relationships in the analytic situation.

Psychoanalytic Case Study

In the following summary of the psychoanalysis of an incest victim, the primary focus will be upon the analysis of the patient's transference of defenses, especially those shared with her parents. Much will therefore have to be omitted.

Opening Phase

Mrs. D, an intelligent professional woman in her late 30s, entered psychoanalysis for treatment of anxiety, depression, insomnia, recent rapid weight gain, "lack of self-confidence," and "feeling too dependent on others for what I think of myself." She was an attractive, although overweight woman who smiled and laughed anxiously a great deal and attempted to make small talk with the analyst. She complained, "I seem to eat as a way of trying to feel more secure." She was ashamed of "crying at the drop of a hat" with no awareness of why she was crying. Her 17-year marriage to a highly domineering, affectionless, and withholding professional man was deteriorating. She was not orgasmic with him. They had adopted two children due to the couple's infertility. She was the oldest of three children and claimed to have had an idyllically happy childhood. Her father had worked as a photographer. Her housewife mother had died three years prior to the analysis.

In her first session, she expressed her reluctance to lie down on the couch and sat on it instead. She handed the analyst a humorous article, which was a short, tongue-in-cheek letter from a psychiatrist to his patient of detailed information for the patient's insurance company. One item was a charge for a replacement for an ashtray and another was for fixing a dent in the wall made by the ashtray. Mrs. D laughingly said that she didn't think she would throw any ashtrays. This proved to be a harbinger of the issue that would later arise around her intense fear of her angry impulses. She presented an initial dream in which she walked into a room full of doctors and their wives for her first appointment with a woman psychiatrist. The psychiatrist kept her waiting, and finally Mrs. D became so angry that she left. Mrs. D's associations included her wish for a female therapist, her fear that the analyst might be a "male chauvinist," her distaste for controlling physicians, and her fear of revealing "deep, dark secrets." The analyst suggested Mrs. D must be worried whether it was safe to expose such "secrets" to him for fear he would either control or ignore her. He added that she seemed to feel ashamed of her wish to back out of the analysis with him, so that in her dream she had resolved these conflicts by, first, having him be a woman and, second, by having him offend her so that she felt justified in leaving. This latter maneuver, seeking offense so that she would then not feel guilty for her own hostility, proved to be characteristic of her and contributed to the eventual demise of her marriage.

In her first year of analysis, she used denial and conscious suppression; she sometimes explicitly refused to free associate if it made her anxious. She frequently asked questions or said that she was thinking but not what she was thinking. With a kind of "pseudoimbecility" (Kramer, 1983) she acted oblivious to the central task of the analysis, and she often filled the hour with material in which she clearly had little affective investment. She felt hurt when the analyst did not answer her questions, tell her what to do, or tell her how she should feel. Such behavior created a role responsiveness pull (Sandler, 1976b) for the analyst to talk more than usual, thereby reassuring her of his interest and concern for her. Similarly, her frequent vagueness, chitchatting, superficiality, Polyannishness, and obviously conscious avoidance of almost anything anxiety-provoking seemed guaranteed to elicit countertransference responses of feeling tantalized, wanting to ask probing questions or to repeatedly confront her, and finally of feeling irritated or bored with her. Her vagueness was typical of the cognitive style of a hysterical personality disorder (Horowitz, 1977). She had numerous dreams full of fog and nebulousness, with herself sometimes tantalizingly half concealed behind veils and gauzy blinds; these dreams simultaneously reflected her "vagueing out" defenses as well as her conflicted wish to entice pursuit and penetration. It became apparent that her major conflictual themes and transferences were often conveyed more in her modes of thinking and interaction than in the content of what she said.

Whenever she had successfully seduced the analyst into asking questions or otherwise probing for clarification, she consciously then experienced him as caring for her. Close attention to her flow of associations, however, revealed that she simultaneously unconsciously perceived him to be controlling and intrusive. The analyst confronted her with how she seemed afraid of linking her thoughts and feelings together in favor of getting the analyst to serve those functions for her. He showed how this perpetuated her feeling inadequate, ill defined, and controlled in the relationship with him, just as she hated feeling with her husband. Gradually, in response to such interpretations, she revealed how she resented her father's hovering, smothering, and subtly coercive behavior. Whenever he came to visit, she constantly felt guilty whenever she wanted to preserve any boundaries in the relationship by not acquiescing to his incessant, seemingly solicitous badgering to reveal why she was in analysis, what she was upset about, the details of her marital life, etc. Accordingly, she felt guilty revealing such a complaint about her father, perceiving herself to be a disloyal daughter to her ostensibly loving and concerned father.

In this context of analyzing her inhibitions against her assertive impulses, she revealed how she had undergone multiple artificial insemination trials. She had hated the bright lights and the way she had to passively allow genital penetration. She had not wanted to become pregnant anyway, but had, like an automaton, done what her husband wanted. She had a nightmare in which, all alone, she gave birth to vermin. In exploring the dream she abreacted a long-repressed memory: at five years of age, her mother had informed her that their already limited times of closeness were coming to an end because she would soon give birth to another child. Mrs. D had shoved her mother, who then fell and later that day suffered a miscarriage. Her parents blamed her for the miscarriage, and the patient felt extremely guilty. Feeling very insecure that night, the patient had crawled into bed with her father and had felt his erection against her. Her father then rejected her, telling her that there was no place for her in their bed. She had felt terribly guilty and evil. This episode had contributed to her developing a massive reaction formation against her aggressive impulses, and yet this important memory clearly served screening functions for what was to emerge later in the analysis.

She revealed her erotic father-transference longings for the analyst in dreams in which he ignored other patients in order to lie on the couch beside her. She wanted a "more personal relationship, not just a doctor-patient relationship" but that seemed "sneaky." At this point, her husband decided to get a divorce, having carried on an affair with another woman. Although the affair had been common knowledge to her two adolescent children, Mrs. D had maintained an amazing unawareness of it, just as for some time she had been unaware of her husband's abusive bullying of their son. She realized in retrospect that there had been many blatant clues of the affair, and she felt like a fool, hurt, enraged, and rejected.

She developed a repetitive cycle of approaching greater conscious awareness of her affectionate and erotic transference feelings, reacting with shame, humiliation, guilt, and anxiety to this awareness. She then would retreat into "muddling up" her thinking, suppressing, withholding, and talking about whatever external, real-life difficulty was available in order to regress once again to a seemingly helpless, dependent position. She felt narcissistically wounded whenever the analyst would not tell her what to do nor take nonanalytic means to reduce her anxiety. When he did not immediately prescribe hypnotics, for example, but instead explored her requesting such medication, she became quite anxious over how intensely angrily she reacted. It became evident that she allowed herself anger only to obliterate "bonds" with people. She experienced herself as "coming apart" as her hatred and vengefulness mounted toward her husband; she felt that she was "losing" herself and would "get stuck" and remain a very "bitter, unloving person" the rest of her life. She painfully realized that she had nothing to show for all the ways she had changed her identity so that her husband would not disapprove of her. Intermittently, she had variations of a recurrent "box dream," occurring when she felt no longer able to "box in" her mounting hateful or erotic impulses. In these nightmares she was enclosed in a box and afraid to get out. Early in the analysis, the dreams involved her huddling panic-stricken in a corner of the box while the walls inexorably closed in upon her.

In her second year of analysis, after fantasizing "stepping over that line" into an "unprofessional" relationship with the analyst, she complained, "I want you to poke more. When I'm bogged down, I want you to poke at me. It really angered me last week that you wouldn't poke." The analyst first empathized with how she experienced him as cold and uncaring if he didn't "poke" by asking questions when she was feeling particularly troubled, and how, in turn, she must feel rejected. He then clarified that she was wanting him to reenact the same controlling and intrusive behavior that she had hated receiving from her father and husband. She became anxious and blurted out,

"What just popped into my head was my father pawing me, and I really feel dirty and guilty. That's how I was feeling when I was bothered by my feelings about you. If my father did something for me, he'd be pawing at me." She stammered that she felt so guilty about wanting the analyst to "poke" her because it felt "like incest." She nevertheless continued to intermittently struggle with the analyst to get him to read her mind, tell her what to do, and to force her to talk about things that she didn't want to discuss, for example, her father's "pawing."

She revealed frequently masturbating while having fantasies of sex with the analyst during the weekend separations: "My sex dreams with you are that I'm the aggressor making love to you, and you're 'there.' It's like I'm experimenting on you." In these fantasies, she frequently initially was the seductress, but then as she became increasingly aroused, such fantasies became too anxiety provoking for her, and she switched to sadomasochistic fantasies of submitting to sex with her husband. On weekends, she often dreamed of having sessions with the analyst in bed.

She derived a "perverse satisfaction" in "tantalizing" the analyst by stating without explanation that her father had "overstepped the boundaries." She vaguely reported that she had frequently walked into her parents' bedroom at "very inopportune times" during her adolescence. She further reported overstimulation: Her parents had openly displayed nudity and entered into the bathroom even when she was occupying it.

She was exquisitely sensitive to anything that suggested that the analyst did not care for her, was coldly exerting power over her, or was not openly communicating verbally. For example, after a session in which she had expressed dismay when the analyst had given her a bill that included a charge for a missed session and he had motioned her toward the couch and suggested that they explore her reaction, she reported the following dream: She had "run things," told the analyst to "shut up" every time he tried to talk, and shoved him down whenever he tried to get up. She had done a "striptease" and had wanted him to beg her to have intercourse. She reported, "You were supposed to lose your composure. Your body would not have lied. I wanted you to say it! It was a power play!" The analyst interpreted her turning passive into active via role reversal as an attempt to salvage her wounded self-esteem and also to retaliate for his perceived domination of her with the gesture and the bill in the previous session.

Continued interpretation of her sexualized form of turning passive into active and her invitation for the analyst to "poke" into her led to her telling about her father sexually molesting her from four to 12 years of age. This had started with his "tickling" her groin and progressed to grueling photography sessions in a studio in which he photographed her nude and masturbated himself and her, sometimes quite roughly. (Only once before, as a teenager, had she informed anyone of the incest. The priest to whom she had talked chastised her severely and told her never again to say such nasty lies about her father, an upstanding citizen of the community.) At this point in her third year of analysis, she experienced disorganizing storms of affect varying from intense anger to extreme shame and guilt. She felt "ugly," "damaged," "slimey," and "perverted." The incest aspect of the father transference was evident in a dream: "I started kissing you passionately. I opened my eyes and your face was fierce and demonic looking. Your body was more like my dad's."

Working Through

Having undergone considerable therapeutic regression, she began her fourth year with complaints that she was a "King junkie." Frightened of her feelings of "enmeshment," she explained that if she felt rejected by the analyst, she wouldn't know who she was and would feel that she was a "bad person." This involved splits in her self and object representations. If she felt unloved by the analyst and, therefore, unlovable, she feared that she would react with intensely destructive rage, hurt the analyst, and permanently lose the loving and caring aspects of herself. Her defensive idealization of her father gradually crumbled. No longer an "inanimate doll" enclosed in a "box" of denial, she relived the incest in a series of trauma dreams and wanted to castrate and kill her father. She transiently developed colitis. She relied upon but felt envious of the analyst's "holding" calmness, complained of his constant "presence" in her mind, and developed an archaic idealizing selfobject transference (Kohut, 1971, 1977). She dreamed of herself as an amoeba who tried to fuse with the analyst, also an amoeba, in order to share the use of his "tough membrane."

The newly developed idealizing transference served multiple purposes. It provided her with enough "sustenance" to tackle the continuing abreaction and working over of the affects of the prolonged incest trauma. Simultaneously, the idealization was a defense against the rage engendered by the earlier father transference as well as her primitive envy. Separations from the analyst made her return to her "box"; she thereby avoided loss of control but felt "empty" and "anchorless." Her "boxing"-herself-in was partially a defense against affects of utter helplessness originally associated with the incest, which she felt unable to tolerate without the analyst's holding function. As a self-soothing transitional phenomenon, she often drove by his office to see if his car was there. For the first time, she confronted her father about the incest. He told her he still had the old photographs and that he intended to keep them to remember their "good times." He pressed her, "Weren't they good times for you?"

When she felt bereft and depersonalized without the analyst, her thoughts turned to her dead mother: "She didn't talk or listen a whole lot. My mom never said 'I love you' to me. You'd kiss her goodnight, and she wouldn't kiss you. The older I got the more distant we got. I felt like an appendage. It was okay if I was or wasn't there. My mother didn't hold me." She could recall her mother hardly ever holding her other than the traumatic time when, as a five-year-old, she had pushed her mother, which in her perception led to one of the mother's many miscarriages. She lamented, "My mental picture of my mother is always of her with her back three-quarters turned to me." Her mother had not allowed Mrs. D to help in the kitchen. She had apparently been unable to tolerate the little girl's inevitable mistakes or messes. Mrs. D recovered from repression memories of her mother "exploding" and viciously and repeatedly pinching her, only to become "super quiet" again afterward. Mrs. D had felt "safe" during her mother's withdrawn states, but also had felt the "most alienated" and "not alive, as though you were safe but a non-entity." Her identification with her mother's intermittently affectless state was evidenced in her self-criticism: "If you're grown up, you're supposed to be emotionless." She gradually began to internalize the analyst's acceptance with that part of herself that felt so dependent and childlike. At long last she began to develop a "sense of safety," and she described her analytic hour as a "sanctuary." The analyst represented the longed-for "good" mother who would have been attentive to her and would have protected her from her father and her own incestuous wishes. She likened the relationship with the analyst to a "protective cocoon" and stated that he was part of her "inner core," that without him she was just a "void."

She had a long, pivotal dream over a weekend: She was very young and small and felt proud of not spilling as she helped herself to raisins and milk. Suddenly, a loud voice berated her, "You can't do anything right! You're just a messy, dirty little girl!" The voice claimed the raisins were "seeds" and chanted, "Needs are the seeds of deeds!" In the dream, Mrs. D then suddenly shifted to her current age and yelled that the voice didn't care about her or it wouldn't have let her father molest her. At that point her father came up behind her and hit her and told her that she couldn't tell anyone. She turned into "an icicle" until she could see the analyst, but when he wouldn't let her cry on his shoulder "the little icicle cracked into little pieces and all went into a little box. It was dead time again." She associated to this dream, "The raisins are all the things I tried to shove back into the box and all the bad things I thought I had done. This voice was very clearly my mother's." She had experienced great difficulty "holding on" over the weekend and had numbed herself to do so (went back into her "box").

The analyst suggested that she must perceive him to be like her mother, unwilling to tolerate "messy" emotions, when she couldn't literally and physically "cry on his shoulder." She hesitantly was doing increasingly more of her own analytic work but often discounted her own interpretations. The analyst interpreted that she must fear that he, too, would discourage her fledgling movement toward autonomy and initiative just as she had perceived her mother to do. He offered the reconstruction that as a young girl she must have come to believe that she was indeed "messy and dirty" and had therefore been so hungry for even the most meager affirmation that she had turned to attempting to please her father. This in turn sowed the "seeds" for the incest "deed." She angrily recalled memories of her mother exploding at her in the kitchen if she ever made a mess. Many of her mental dialogues with the analyst outside of sessions were of acting like a "two-year-old brat" and wanting the analyst to set limits. The analyst suggested that she associate "caring" with her mother's angry undermining of her striving for autonomy.

A cycle developed in which she attacked the analyst with guilt-inducing criticisms, attempting to coerce him into giving advice, only to feel that she was going to "explode" with hatred when he maintained the analytic stance, followed by her shifting back to the father transference with punishing trauma dreams in which the analyst/her father sadistically masturbated her. After such events she berated herself with messages that the analyst interpreted as introjected from her parents: "Act nice or no one's going to want to be with you. Don't cry or I'll give you something to cry about!" Continued working through of her conflicts over aggression, assertiveness, and initiative led to her making a major career shift to a more responsible and higher paying position.

She frequently was angry with the analyst as she blamed him for the loss of her idealized illusion of her mother. She realized she had felt like an inanimate "mechanical doll" with her mother. Memories cropped up of coming home from school and wanting to talk to her mother, only to recurrently hear her mother say, "Not now, I'm too busy." Her mother had always seemed either disapproving or "too busy." She recalled episodes of such gross insensitivity and lack of empathy on her mother's part that even Mrs. D's father had felt embarrassed. For example, the mother routinely subjected any guests to seemingly thoughtless insults. Mrs. D suspected that such thoughtlessness was not without malice.

At this time, during a visit from her father, a significant aspect of her pathological relationship with him became clear. During the visit, her father constantly wanted hugs and kisses. Mrs. D felt very uncomfortable giving this physical affection, but if she attempted to avoid it, her father whined, "No kiss for your dad?" Out of guilt Mrs. D therefore kissed him even though inwardly she rebelled. She knew that if she refused, he would seem so hurt that she would then feel very guilty. This was a type of projective identification in which the "rules" were that neither one was to be aware of or openly express hostility toward the other, the "object of the game" being for him to control her or else to make her "pay" by being the one who carried the burden and stigma of all the hurtfulness and hatefulness, leaving the perpetrator blameless.

This pattern cast light upon a phenomenon in the analysis. She felt angry when the analyst did not answer her "friendly" probing personal questions, and she fantasied walking out. The analyst showed her how, with her seemingly harmless questions, she wanted to coerce him into letting her cross the analytic boundary or else she would feel hurt and he was to feel guilty. He interpreted her repeating through role reversal, turning passive into active, and identification with the aggressor, the same situation in which she was victimized by her father in order to gain revenge against and control over the analyst/her father. This pattern was part of a cycle: If she felt threatened by the intensity of her sexual urges toward the analyst or her wish to merge with him, she attempted to counter such "enmeshment" with distancing, "chatter," or hostility, only to reexperience the dreaded "dead" or "mechanical doll" feelings, in turn blaming him for the "disconnection" and projecting and displacing her hostility onto the analyst, and finally attempting to coerce him into reestablishing for her the libidinal tie she had disrupted. If he confronted rather than actualized the role enactment, she then erupted in anger and experienced the intrapsychic obliteration of the protective selfobject analyst with a shift to the sadistic father transference, again experiencing incest dreams. Becoming aware of her aggression jolted her. She lamented that she had spent her life not knowing what she felt, just pretending what she thought she should feel.

Such work led to her again confronting her father about the incest. He once again told her, "I thought you liked it." She felt repulsed by how aroused she felt by a series of sadomasochistic rape dreams. She associated to her disturbing masturbation fantasies that started pleasantly with the analyst but ended up violently, but arousingly, with her father. These fantasies and dreams were interpreted as her turning passive into active to defend against the helplessness associated with the incest memories. They were compromise formations simultaneously punishing her for her incestuous transference urges and defending against her "owning" such feelings toward the analyst in the present. Typically after such intense work she felt "scattered and so afraid, alone and in a vacuum," as though she had lost her mother.

She simultaneously wished to be the analyst's wife and his child. She worried the analyst would "go away." This chronic insecurity, so evident in the transference, led the analyst to remember one of the patient's early memories: Her mother had lost her in a large public park when Mrs. D was a preschooler. Using this and other recollections, he suggested that Mrs. D was afraid that he could easily and at any time forget all about her and simply not even think about her, just as she must have experienced her mother. This reconstruction was confirmed by her immediately developing a dissociative state in which she was overwhelmed by feelings of utter helplessness followed by disorganizing rage toward the analyst/her mother. She recalled other incidents of having been "forgotten." In discussions with her younger brother, she discovered that he, too, had been repeatedly forgotten; for example, the parents often failed to pick him up after church and school events. Mrs. D further lost her "gilded" image of her mother, cried in despair, and once again experienced "that closed down, dead feeling." She rebounded from this by plaguing the analyst with questions and demands, which he interpreted as indicative of her need to "get a response" from him/her "not-there" transference mother. She acknowledged she wanted to anger him; her enraged mother's vicious pinching was preferable to her withdrawn "absence."

Mrs. D's most fragmented, tumultuous, and deeply regressed moments came during this working through of her chronic sense of unimportance, unlovability, and rage in the relationship with her mother. As she gradually disidentified with her mother's oscillations between emotional deadness and abusive rage, she developed greater empathy for that devastated part of herself that had felt responsible for her mother's rage, unworthy of her mother's affirmation, and deserving of her father's abuse.

Associated with her isolated-off affects were split-off fragments of her self and object representations, which contributed toward oscillating transference states. One of the more difficult aspects of the analysis of her incest experience involved her sense of guilt and responsibility for the incest because, at times, she had felt sexually aroused. This meant to her that her father must have indeed been correct and that she had liked it and initiated it. Partially because of the chronic deprivation and lack of emotional "connectedness" with her mother, she felt terribly needy of experiencing a sense of intimacy, closeness, and nurturance with the analyst. She also had an intense desire for the analyst to be an idealized new object, the good mother and father rolled together, that she felt she had never experienced. Her desperately desired sense of the analytic relationship as a safe haven, as a holding relationship (Winnicott, 1975) uncontaminated by lustful, incestuous impulses or messy emotional needs was always threatened whenever she again became increasingly aware of sexual desires for the analyst or wishes to merge with him. At such times she would resort to "chit-chatting"; in keeping with her activation of suppression, denial, and Polyannishness, she activated the "pseudostupid" aspect of her self-representation. Whenever she did this, she disconnected herself both from the analyst and from her own affective life.

This destruction of meaning in the analytic relationship and the creation of massive barriers to communication is what Modell (1984) calls "affective nonrelatedness" and Langs (1978, 1981) describes as a "Type C communicative field." In cutting off any feeling of connectedness to the analyst, she reexperienced feelings of emotional deadness associated with that aspect of her self-representation that felt unloved and unattended to by her mother. This state, of course, was very painful, and she terminated it by angrily attacking the analyst, blaming him for having disconnected from her. This shift to the abandoning mother transference involved the type of two-tiered projective identification described by Kernberg (1987) and Porder (1988). The conscious aspect of her activated internalized object relationship was of the analyst as the abandoning, uncaring, nonprotective mother and of herself as the aggrieved, neglected, hurt, and justifiably angry child. Simultaneously, the unconscious aspect of the object relationship then enacted in the analytic relationship involved a role reversal and identification with the aggressor in which she played the role of her explosive, rejecting, and pinching mother, whereas the analyst was made to feel like a guilty, anxious child under attack.

Termination Phase

In the final phase of her analysis she became alive emotionally, as evidenced by changes in her "box dreams." They occurred less frequently, and she finally climbed out of the "box." She developed a sense that she had a "home inside," even during separations from the analyst, and that "there was someone there inside after all." Showing good capacity to understand her conflicts and emotions, she no longer "vagued-out" nor used denial so extensively. Her dealings with the analyst as well as family members, employers, and supervisors became marked by straightforwardness and assertiveness. She developed the capacity to tolerate intense affects.

During her eighth year of analysis, she recovered previously repressed painfully traumatic memories of the incest. To help herself prevent fragmentation, she wrote her perception of the incest experience. The following excerpts illustrate the brainwashing, the induction of guilt, the background of deprivation, and the oscillation of extreme overstimulation and terror with moments of soothing that are so characteristic of "soul murder" (Shengold, 1979).

> Is it really Daddy? Soon, big hands are stroking me, feathering touches that flame. It feels good and I'm scared. I want it to stop—I want it to continue. In and out, in and out, Faster, slower.
>
> "Pretty little baby. You know it feels so good. Pretty little hole, pretty little finger, pretty little girl. You know you like it. Show me how you like it. Tell me how you like it. Tell me how it feels so good. Pretty little baby." I tell him it hurts. He says, "It doesn't hurt, you like it, see how wet you are." I nod, anxious to placate.
>
> He comes to the side of the table and gently combs my hair with his fingers. I am happy because Daddy is back and it is finished. He takes his hand away. I feel bereft and curl towards him.
>
> I call out to Daddy and there is no answer, only the rasping sighs. I cry out again. My sobs are choked by his penis in my mouth. I am being crushed between his hand clamping my head and his fingers in my vagina, much thicker than any stick, and rough with their frantic movement.
>
> I cannot move—I cannot breathe! I struggle, fighting for air, and exploding pain zaps through me. Maybe if I lay still, it will go away. I CANNOT BREATHE! The thrusting piston in my mouth erupts and he tells me, "Swallow, little one, swallow. Taste how good it is. Swallow, pretty baby."
>
> I feel skittish, alert to new assaults, but his gentle touches and soothing murmurs gradually ease my tension. He talks to me, telling me how special Daddy's little girl is and how we have this secret only we can share. He cups my pubis, demands I will tell no one, stabs me hard with his finger, and lightly strokes me until I am trembling. I agree.

> I once overheard my mother tell my father she enjoyed the days he "took me to the park because I was always so quiet and well-behaved after playing so hard."

With the reference to her mother, she crumbled up the paper, violently sobbed out, "She had to know!" and hurled the paper across the room.

During her termination phase, Mrs. D began to experience the flowering of previously latent talents for writing poetry. After termination, this subliminatory outlet has continued to flourish, and she has used the poetry to further place her incest experience into perspective. She has continued to rise to positions of higher responsibility at her place of employment. She remains conflicted about again involving herself in heterosexual relationships, but is considering dating again. She enjoys close, excellent relations with her young adult children.

Discussion

Mrs. D evidenced many features commonly associated with father-daughter incest, including feelings of guilt over her "oedipal victory," a profound sense of shame, self-loathing, and perversion, and a sense of blame for the incest because at times she had felt quite sexually aroused during it and because, once "trained" by her father, she had sometimes initiated the incestuous overtures when she had felt insecure about her father's love. Through turning passive into active and blaming herself for the incest, she attempted to achieve a modicum of mastery over the trauma, and this allowed her to maintain an idealized attitude toward her father and to accept the incest as an expression of his "love."

With the advent of ego psychology, modern-day psychoanalysts have come to view the recovery of memories not as the goal of psychoanalysis but rather as a by-product of the unfolding of a successful psychoanalytic process (Arlow, 1986). In this case it was evident relatively early in the analysis that Mrs. D probably had experienced incest. She certainly made it tempting to ask questions probing for it and to pressure her to stop concealing the obviously important details about her father "pawing" her. For the analyst to have fallen prey to these temptations, however, would have been for him to have simply bypassed or interfered with Mrs. D's resistances rather than analyzing them, and, more importantly, to have fallen into the trap of enacting with her once again the scene of the abuser coercing the abused. Pursuit of content, namely, memories and details, at this point would have been colluding with the patient in maintaining what Langs (1978,

1981) calls a "Type B field," characterized by the major communications being conveyed nonverbally and through projective identification. Her major defenses against awareness of the impact the incestuous relationship had had upon her did not involve repression. She had been well aware of the fact of incest throughout her life, as were most of Soll's cases (1984), but had massively isolated the affects of helplessness, rage, terror, and sexual arousal. This involved a "vertical split," in which much of the affective life of her childhood was walled off (see also Shengold, 1979). This split was maintained by her massive denial. Here we do not mean to imply that she disavowed that the incest had ever happened; rather, she denied the meaning of the incest.

Incest is not simply an event; it involves an incestuous *relationship* within a family milieu that denies the presence, meaning, and impact of the abuse. Usually in such a family relationship, incestuous behavior has occurred over a prolonged period of time, and these chronic traumatic relationships lead the patient to develop characterologically entrenched defenses, an "accommodation syndrome" (Summit, 1983a, 1983b), that further interferes with development long after the incest has ended. Thus, what the incest patient repeats and transfers via enactment in the therapeutic situation is not just the trauma, but also his or her defenses against the affects and meanings associated with the traumatic relationships.

In works exploring the concept of denial, Dorpat (1983, 1985) has advocated the use of the term in the manner we are here employing it. In earlier papers, Dorpat (1985, 1989) and King (1988) have proposed that in cases of trauma, this denial of the meaning of the trauma may involve failure to achieve symbolic representation of aspects of the trauma. These aspects of the traumatic experience and the traumatic relationship are largely communicated via enactment, namely, interactional repetition compulsion (Dorpat, 1988). Mrs. D communicated many aspects of the incestuous relationship via her unconscious pressures upon the analyst for him to "probe" and "push" into her. As the initial father transference unfolded, aspects of her repetition compulsion included attempts to induce within the analyst a complementary countertransference identification with her father (Racker, 1968) to control, subvert, and penetrate her as had her father. It was largely through the consistent confrontation and clarification of these coercive tactics and role responsiveness pressures (Sandler, 1976b) that ultimately led Mrs. D, after two years of analysis, to openly reveal her incestuous past.

Our claim is that an important aspect of a child's responses to psychic trauma is determined not only by the traumatic event itself, but also by the parents' response to the child's reactions to the event. Our hypothesis regarding the negative effects of prolonged parental denial and neglect is supported by the studies of Balint (1969) and Bowlby (1988).

Balint (1969) emphasizes the importance of the parents' response to psychic traumas to the children. Parental indifference and neglect of their child's needs for assistance in mastering trauma play a central role in the maintenance and intensification of the child's psychopathological responses to trauma.

Bowlby (1988) highlights the psychopathology that results in children when they are pressed by their parents to deny or repress certain traumatic events. The task of the therapist, according to Bowlby, is to bring these events to light and to assist the patient to understand and integrate the thoughts, feelings, and behaviors that the traumatic events elicited.

Part of what Mrs. D enacted involved defenses shared with her father. Her "muddling up" and "vagueing out" were not just seductive invitations for the analyst to intrude, but they also were manifestations of a childhood full of adaptation to her father's "brainwashing" of her. He had actively interfered with her developing a capacity to perceive her own emotions by telling her what she was supposed to feel and punishing her whenever she even tentatively suggested that she felt otherwise. The father, the son of a pious, domineering, fundamentalist Protestant minister, in order to disavow his guilt, apparently needed to believe that his abusive and intrusive behavior was an expression of his love for Mrs. D and that she enjoyed it. He therefore insisted that Mrs. D also not perceive or speak about his destructive aggression. In this family where parents walked around nude, entered the bathroom when Mrs. D was using it, and committed incest, there was never any cognitive sexual education—sexual impulses were acted upon rather than spoken of. Mrs. D's mother didn't even prepare her child for menstruation. Mrs. D's "muddling up" her thinking whenever early in the analysis issues of aggression or sexuality came to the fore represented a pervasive identification with this aspect of her father's defenses. Her identification with the aggressor had included identifying with his denial of his hostility. Similarly, she had defensively identified with his mode of projective identification, whereby anyone who dared perceive and confront his hostile intent was made to feel all of the guilt that the aggressor could not tolerate experiencing. Thus, what Mrs. D repeated or enacted in the analysis was not just the trauma of the incest, but also both the defenses she had developed against the meanings and affects associated with the incest and the defenses of the perpetrator. Originally described by Ferenczi (1933), this sharing of defenses through identification by the traumatized victim with the traumatizer has more recently been explored by Blum (1986, 1987).

Often the father-daughter incest victim experiences the greatest unconscious rage toward her mother. The patient frequently massively defends against awareness of such rage. By the time such rage begins to surface in the treatment, the patient already feels that she has lost her father, and she doesn't want to lose her mother as well. In other words, as the patient's denial, repression, and idealization crumble, her ability to hold onto the capacity to evoke any loving and self-sustaining aspects of her mother's object representation is swept away with the unleashing of her previously walled-off rage. This then leads to a state of emptiness and loss. Such intensely destructive rage is overdetermined.

The mother's inability or unwillingness to protect her daughter is but one source of the victim's rage. In our experience as well as that of others (Furman & Furman, 1984a, 1984b; Ganzarain, 1989), there is often a seriously impaired mother-child relationship even before the incest occurred. The deficits in the dyadic relationship often contribute to the daughter turning to the father for comfort, affection, and protection. The girl's oedipal relationships are thus shaped not only by competitiveness toward the mother, but also by resentment toward her arising from chronic disappointment. One relatively common pathogenic factor in the incest victim's relationship with her mother is what Furman and Furman (1984a, 1984b) have called "intermittent decathexis." This is a type of parental dysfunction in which the parent is prone to periodically neglect and/or fail to attend to the child's welfare, leading to repeated strain and shock traumata (Kris, 1956) such as the child becoming lost and forgotten, incurring abuse, or having accidents. The child tends to identify with the parents' intermittent decathexis and thus relates similarly as an adult to her children and, in treatment, to her analyst. The deficits in the mother-daughter relationship therefore can lead to a variety of countertransference pulls. The analyst may feel decathected, that is, unimportant, irrelevant, or ignored. He or she may feel mistrusted.

Phases of deep regression in successful treatment may involve intense dependency on the analyst as a new and corrective archaic mother figure or selfobject (Kohut, 1971, 1977), and then the analyst may experience a strong pull to avoid the patient's devastating despair and rage that can cataclysmically erupt from even a minor disappointment. However, during disruptions in the selfobject transference, it is especially the analysis of the negative transference that contributes to mutative interpretations and reconstruction of the damaging effects of the mother-daughter relationship. This level of work is just as important as analyzing the effects of the incestuous father-daughter relationship. Such work cannot adequately ensue in many of the short-term treatment modalities most often available to incest victims. Nor can it occur in psychoanalytic therapy if the analyst cannot tolerate being perceived as a neglectful, uncaring mother.

Summary

A survey of the psychoanalysis of a woman who had experienced incest with her father from prelatency into preadolescence is presented. Her denial of her father's hostility was overdetermined. To deny how badly she suffered, she also needed to deny his hostility. This denial had an interactional component; she denied the vicious destructive aspect of the incest as her father did and in unconscious collusion with him. Such denial also allowed her to hold onto the nurturing, caring aspect of her father; she desperately needed to do this to compensate for her sense of unlovability in the relationship with her mother, to ward off the psychic disintegration she experienced with awareness of her overwhelming rage, and to adapt to her father's demands and brainwashing. A crucial aspect of the clinical work involved the analysis of defenses she had developed in complementary reaction to her parents' defenses.

As she abreacted and worked through the incest trauma, she underwent a further regressive shift to a primitive idealizing selfobject transference. During that phase she created tremendous pressures on the analyst to take care of her and protect her from the painful and disorganizing affects as she wished her mother had done on the one hand, or, if that failed, to punish her as her mother had so often done.

All too often, many of the current approaches to working with incest victims emphasize uncovering and abreacting the incest trauma, blaming the perpetrator, and not thoroughly analyzing the negative transferences. As Blum (1986) has put it, "Shock trauma, for example, seduction, could also be a seductively simple explanation, given overdetermination and long-standing pathogenic patterns as in child abuse and neglect." Mrs. D, for example, was probably as devastated by the chronic sense of being an unwanted, easily lost and forgotten, unlovable burden to her depressed and frequently emotionally absent mother as she was by the admittedly damaging incest experience. The failure in the mother's holding and mirroring functions set the stage for the incest and permitted it to go on for an extended time.

Analyzing the relationship context of the incest was more difficult but just as important as analyzing the direct incest impact. However, the seduction theory and the abreaction model continue to be used inappropriately, and all too often therapists react to hints of incest in a patient's past with probing questions. We advocate great care or avoidance of this technical stance. In Mrs. D's case, it would have represented the analyst's having been seduced into enacting with the patient another version of the incestuous object relationship. Such an active and directive technical approach would also have interfered with the analysis of the crucially important negative transference when Mrs. D experienced the analyst's abstinence as though he were the uncaring and "not there" mother during the later stages of the analysis. When a child has been forced to share and identify with pathological defenses of the parents, as Mrs. D was made to do, there is a tendency for the patient through projective identification to behaviorally induce the analyst to once again share those defenses.

References

Abraham, K. (1907). On the significance of sexual traumas in childhood for the symptomatology of dementia praecox. In *Clinical papers and essays on psychoanalysis* (pp. 13–20). New York: Basic Books, 1955.

Arlow, J. (1986). The relation of theories of pathogenesis to psychoanalytic therapy. In A. Richards & M. Willick (Eds.), *Psychoanalysis: The science of mental conflict* (pp. 49–64). Hillsdale, NJ: Analytic Press.

Balint, M. (1969). Trauma and object relationship. *International Journal of Psycho-Analysis, 50,* 429–435.

Bernstein, A. E. (1989). Analysis of two adult female patients who have been victims of incest in childhood. *Journal of the American Academy of Psychoanalysis, 17,* 207–221.

Blum, H. (1986). The concept of the reconstruction of trauma. In A. Rothstein (Ed.), *The reconstruction of trauma: Its significance in clinical work* (pp. 7–28). Madison, CT: International Universities Press.

Blum, H. (1987). The role of identification in the resolution of trauma. *Psychoanalytic Quarterly, 56,* 609–627.

Bonaparte, M. (1953). *Female sexuality.* New York: International Universities Press.

Bowlby, J. (1988). *A secure base: Parent-child attachment and healthy human development.* New York: Basic Books.

Braun, B. (1984). Towards a theory of multiple personality and other dissociative phenomena. *Psychiatric Clinics of North America, 7,* 171–193.

Breuer, J., & Freud, S. (1895). Studies on hysteria. *Standard edition of the complete psychological works of Sigmund Freud, 2,* 1–305. London: Hogarth Press, 1953.

Briere, J., & Zaidi, L. (1989). Sexual abuse histories and sequelae in female psychiatric emergency room patients. *American Journal of Psychiatry, 146,* 1602–1606.

Brooks, B. (1982). Familial influences in father-daughter incest. *Journal of Psychiatric Treatment and Evaluation, 4,* 117–124.

Bryer, J., Nelson, B., Miller, J., & Krol, P. (1987). Childhood sexual and physical abuse as factors in adult psychiatric illness. *American Journal of Psychiatry, 144,* 1426–1430.

Chu, J., & Dill, D. L. (1990). Dissociative symptoms in relation to childhood physical and sexual abuse. *American Journal of Psychiatry, 147,* 887–892.

Dewald, P. (1989). Effects on an adult of incest in childhood: A case report. *Journal of the American Psychoanalytic Association, 37,* 997–1014.

Dorpat, T. L. (1983). Denial, defect, symptom formation—and construction. *Psychoanalytic Inquiry, 3,* 223–253.

Dorpat, T. L. (1985). *Denial and defense in the therapeutic situation.* New York: Jason Aronson.

Dorpat, T. L. (1988). Self-fulfilling prophecies and the repetition compulsion: An interactional perspective. Paper presented to the Seattle Psychoanalytic Society.

Dorpat, T. L. (1989). Some relationships between psychic trauma and defense. Paper presented at Child and Adolescent Victims of Trauma Symposium, Seattle.

Ferenczi, S. (1933). Confusion of tongues between adults and the child. In M. Balint (Ed.), *Final contributions to the problems and methods of psychoanalysis* (pp. 156–167). London: Hogarth Press, 1955.

Finkelhor, D. (1979). *Sexually victimized children.* New York: Free Press.

Flugel, J. (1953). *The psychoanalytic study of the family.* London: Hogarth Press.

Freud, A. (1936). The ego and the mechanisms of defense. In *The writings of Anna Freud* (Vol. 2). New York: International Universities Press.

Freud, A. (1981). A psychoanalyst's view of sexual abuse by parents. In P. B. Mrazek & C. H. Kempe (Eds.), *Sexually abused children and their families* (pp. 33–34).

Freud, S. (1914). On the history of the psychoanalytic movement. *Standard Edition, 14,* 7–66. London: Hogarth Press, 1963.

Freud, S. (1917). Introductory lectures on psycho-analysis. *Standard Edition, 15 and 16.* London: Hogarth Press, 1963.

Freud, S. (1918). From the history of an infantile neurosis. *Standard Edition, 17,* 7–123. London: Hogarth Press, 1955.

Freud, S. (1933). New introductory lectures on psychoanalysis. *Standard Edition, 22,* 1–182. London: Hogarth Press, 1964.

Furman, E. (1956). An ego disturbance in a young child. *Psychoanalytic Study of the Child, 11,* 312–335.

Furman, E. (1989). Discussion at the Annual Hanna Perkins Symposium, Cleveland.

Furman, R., & Furman, E. (1984a). Intermittent decathexis: A type of parental dysfunction. *International Journal of Psycho-Analysis, 65,* 423–434.

Furman, R., & Furman, E. (1984b). Panel: The Seduction Hypothesis. American Psychoanalytic Association Meeting, New York.

Ganzarain, R. C. (1989). Contribution to discussion group: When Incest Is the Issue: Transference and Countertransference. American Psychoanalytic Association meeting.

Ganzarain, R. C., & Buchele, B. J. (1989). *Fugitives of incest: A perspective from psychoanalysis and groups.* Madison, CT: International Universities Press.

Gillman, R. D. (1986). Physical trauma and actual seduction. In A. Rothstein (Ed.), *The reconstruction of trauma: Its significance in clinical work* (pp. 73–94). Madison, CT: International Universities Press.

Goodwin, J., McCarty, T., & DiVasto, P. (1981). Prior incest in abusive mothers. *Child Abuse and Neglect, 5,* 1–9.

Gross, R. J., Doerr, H., Caldirola, D., Guzinski, G. M., & Ripley, H. S. (1980–81). Borderline syndrome and incest in chronic pain patients. *International Journal of Psychiatry in Medicine, 10,* 79–98.

Herman, J. L. (1981). *Father-daughter incest.* Cambridge, MA: Harvard University Press.

Herman, J. L. (1986). Histories of violence in an outpatient population: An exploratory study. *American Journal of Orthopsychiatry, 56,* 137–141.

Herman, J. L., Perry, J. C., & van der Kolk, B. A. (1988). Childhood trauma in borderline personality disorder. Unpublished manuscript.

Horowitz, M. J. (Ed.) (1977). *Hysterical personality.* New York: Jason Aronson.

Katan, A. (1973). Children who were raped. *Psychoanalytic Study of the Child, 28,* 208–224.

Kernberg, O. F. (1976). *Object relations theory and clinical psychoanalysis.* New York: Jason Aronson.

Kernberg, O. F. (1987). Projection and projective identification: Developmental and clinical aspects. In J. Sandler (Ed.), *Projection, identification, projective identification* (pp. 93–116). Madison, CT: International Universities Press.

King, K. R. (1988). Early childhood trauma and the repetition compulsion: A developmental object relations perspective. Paper presented to Section of Psychiatry, British Columbia Medical Association Meeting.

Kluft, R. P. (Ed.) (1989). Treatment of victims of sexual abuse. *Psychiatric Clinics of North American, 12.*

Kohut, H. (1971). *The analysis of the self.* New York: International Universities Press.

Kohut, H. (1977). *The restoration of the self.* New York: International Universities Press.

Kramer, S. (1983). Object-coercive doubting: A pathological defensive response to maternal incest. *Journal of the American Psychoanalytic Association, 31* (Suppl.), 325–352.

Kris, E. (1956). The recovery of childhood memories in psychoanalysis. *Psychoanalytic Study of the Child, 11,* 54–88.

Langs, R. (1978). Some communicative properties of the bi-personal field. *International Journal of Psychoanalytic Psychotherapy, 7,* 89–161.

Langs, R. (1981). Modes of "cure" in psychoanalysis and psychoanalytic psychotherapy. *International Journal of Psycho-Analysis, 62,* 199–214.

Levine, H. (Ed.) (1990). *Adult analysis and childhood sexual abuse.* Hillsdale, NJ: Analytic Press.

Margolis, M. (1977). A preliminary report of a case of consummated mother-son incest. *Annual of Psychoanalysis, 5,* 267–293.

Margolis, M. (1984). A case of mother-adolescent son incest: A follow-up study. *Psychoanalytic Quarterly, 53,* 355–385.

Modell, A. (1984). *Psychoanalysis in a new context.* New York: International Universities Press.

Molnar, G., & Cameron, P. (1975). Incest syndromes: Observations in a general hospital psychiatric unit. *Canadian Psychiatric Association Journal, 20,* 373–377.

Mrazek, P. B., & Kempe, C. H. (1981). *Sexually abused children and their families.* New York: Pergamon Press.

Ogata, S., Silk, K., Goodrich, S., Lohr, N., Westen, D., & Hill, E. (1990). Childhood sexual and physical abuse in adult patients with borderline personality disorders. *American Journal of Psychiatry, 147,* 1008–1013.

Porder, M. S. (1988). Projective identification: An alternative hypothesis. *Psychoanalytic Quarterly, 56,* 431–451.

Rachman, A. W. (1989). Confusion of tongues: The Ferenczian metaphor for childhood seduction and emotional trauma. *Journal of the American Academy of Psychoanalysis, 17,* 181–205.

Racker, H. (1968). *Transference and countertransference.* New York: International Universities Press.

Rascovsky, M., & Rascovsky, A. (1950). On consummated incest. *International Journal of Psychoanalysis, 31,* 42–47.

Reich, A. (1932). Analysis of a case of brother-sister incest. In *Annie Reich: Psychoanalytic contributions* (pp. 288–311). New York: International Universities Press, 1973.

Richards, A. D. (1988). Self-mutilation and father-daughter incest: A psychoanalytic case report. In H. P. Blum, Y. Kramer, A. K. Richards, & A. D. Richards (Eds.), *Fantasy, myth and reality: Essays in honor of Jacob A. Arlow, M.D.* (pp. 465–478). Madison, CT: International Universities Press.

Russell, D. E. H. (1986). *The secret trauma.* New York: Basic Books.

Sandler, J. (1976a). Actualization and object relationships. *Journal of the Philadelphia Association of Psychoanalysis, 3,* 59–70.

Sandler, J. (1976b). Countertransference and role-responsiveness. *International Review of Psycho-Analysis, 3,* 43–70.

Sandler, J., & Sandler, A. M. (1978). On the development of object relationships and affects. *International Journal of Psycho-Analysis, 59,* 285–296.

Shengold, L. (1979). Child abuse and deprivation: Soul murder. *Journal of the American Psychoanalytic Association, 27,* 533–560.

Shengold, L. (1980). Some reflections on a case of mother-adolescent son incest. *International Journal of Psycho-Analysis, 61,* 461–476.

Simpson, C., & Porter, G. (1981). Self-mutilation in children and adolescents. *Bulletin of the Menninger Clinic, 45,* 428–438.

Soll, M. (1984). The transferable penis and the self representation. *International Journal of Psychoanalytic Psychotherapy, 10,* 473–494.

Steele, B., & Alexander, H. (1981). Long-term effects of sexual abuse in childhood. In P. B. Mrazek & C. H. Kempe (Eds.), *Sexually abused children and their families.* New York: Pergamon Press.

Stone, M. H. (1981). Borderline syndromes: A consideration of subtypes and an overview: Directions for research. *Psychiatric Clinics of North American, 4,* 3–13.

Stone, M. H. (1989a). Incest in borderline patients. In R. Kluft (Ed.), *Incest and multiple personality.* Washington, DC: American Psychiatric Press.

Stone, M. H. (1989b). Individual psychotherapy with victims of incest. *Psychiatric Clinics of North America, 12,* 237–255.

Summit, R. (1983a). The child sexual abuse accommodation syndrome. *Child Abuse and Neglect, 7,* 177–193.

Summit, R. (1983b). Recognition and treatment of child sexual abuse. In C. Hollingworth (Ed.), *Coping with pediatric illness.* New York: Spectrum.

van der Kolk, B. (1989, February 24). Traumatic antecedents of borderline personality. Paper presented at Pacific Northwest Trauma Symposium II, Seattle.

van Leeuwen, K. (1988). Resistances in the treatment of a sexually molested 6-year-old girl. *International Review of Psycho-Analysis, 15,* 149–156.

Westen, D., Ludolph, P., Misle, B., Ruffins, S., & Block, J. (1990). Physical and sexual abuse in adolescent girls with borderline personality disorders. *American Journal of Orthopsychiatry, 60,* 55–66.

Williams, M. (1987). Reconstruction of an early seduction and its aftereffects. *Journal of the American Psychoanalytic Association, 35,* 145–163.

Winnicott, D. W. (1975). *Through paediatrics to psycho-analysis.* New York: Basic Books.

Woodbury, J., & Schwartz, E. (1971). *The silent sin.* New York: Signet Books.

Zanarini, M., Gunderson, J., Marino, M., et al. (1989). Childhood experiences of borderline patients. *Comprehensive Psychiatry, 30,* 18–25.

Zaslow, S. L. (1988). Comments on "Confusion of tongues." *Contemporary Psychoanalysis, 24,* 211–225.

Zivney, O. A., Nash, M. R., & Hulsey, T. L. (1988). Sexual abuse in early versus late childhood: Differing patterns of pathology as revealed on the Rorschach. *Psychotherapy, 25,* 99–106.

Aspects of Homosexuality

Florence Holland

The homosexual, male and female, whether overt, latent, or a dweller on infinitely undulating, vaguely delineated borderlands, is surely a paradigm of universal human ambivalence. When Freud asked, "What does she [woman] want?" he might have turned to the homosexual for further befuddlement, and, next, to the student of the subject. Beginning with Freud's (1905) doubts of neurosis or psychosis in the homosexual—"Many people are abnormal in their sexual life who in every other respect approximate to the average" (p. 37)—and proceeding through recent literature, agreement, even tentative, is hard to come by. There are those who hold that the overt homosexual is psychotic, ipso facto and no nonsense about it. Alexander states perversions are "partial psychoses" and Bychowski that homosexuality is close to psychosis because of the use of primitive defense mechanisms (Wiedeman, 1962). Then there are more or less current writers who adhere to Freud's less adamant, less categorizing opinions: Socarides (1962) holds that homosexuality, especially the female variety, represents neither neurosis nor psychosis per se, but may accompany, exacerbate, or defend against both neurosis and psychosis.

Thus the topic of homosexuality, like the homosexual himself, appears as a palimpsest; whatever is faintly legible thereon is overlaid and underlaid with older and newer writings, shades and shadows. Bergler (1957) defines homosexuality as a "neurotic disease which damages the whole personality." I find the obverse more acceptable: that homosexuality would follow damage to the personality. Wiedeman (1962) concludes that homosexuals may have impaired or intact ego with splitting usually present. This writer will not hold, in the current mode of "cop-out," that the truth lies "somewhere between," for that is meaningless. I believe that this truth does not as yet lie within our grasp. For many years I worked closely with female homosexuals—both inmates and staff members at the New York City Department of Correction's House of Detention for Women. I also have friends who are homosexual, male and female. It is this experience and reading of our literature that constitute the raw material of this paper. There will be no attempt at final definition of homosexuality or its assignment to categories of psychic disease or normality.

On the etiology of homosexuality there is more agreement than on definition. Freud, in "The Psychogenesis of a Case of Homosexuality in a Woman" (1920) postulates an *inborn* quality (which quality we probably should refer today to universal infantile bisexuality) and, in the same paper, advocates the use of treatment by *surgery* rather than by psychoanalysis as more efficacious. The latter reflects his then view that some species of hermaphroditism might be present. He concluded that considerable latent homosexuality exists in all (normal, heterosexual) people and that (male) homosexuality is strongly determined by fixation to the mother. This is still accepted (with the addition that female homosexuals are also fixated to the mother), as his theory of abnormal resolution of the oedipal situation is still accepted. He pointed out that, although denigrated by his patient, the role of her father in the etiology of her homosexual outcome was crucial. The role of the father will be one of the main points in my paper.

Just as many writers have cited "castration shock" (the discovery of the lack of a penis and consequent fear of and disgust with female genitalia) in the male homosexual, Fenichel (1945) states that the sight of a penis may create fear of violation in the incipient female homosexual (p. 338). Fixation to the mother is cited by most writers (Bergler, 1957; Fenichel, 1945; Socarides, 1962). Pasche adds that the mother in these cases does not acknowledge the authority of the father (Gillespie, 1964). This factor, too, is an important one in the cases of female homosexuality presented in this paper. Jacobson (1964) states that in some manifest homosexuals, male and female, identification is with an active "phallic" mother; this identification has permitted their egos to develop sufficient stability, functional ability, to build up a comparatively consistent and coherent concept of their self (p. 22). My cases will describe two homosexual women who held responsible jobs and managed their lives with reasonable success and one who failed in both directions.

While much of Freud's thinking is still valid and invaluable, some of the concepts such as organicity as a factor should be discarded, as he himself pointed out that femininity and masculinity, sexual passivity or aggressiveness, were not determining elements in the homosexual or heterosexual outcome. For organicity, we might substitute the defense of denial—denial of the plain fact of one's own genital maleness or femaleness. In more current terms, we see "fixation to the mother" in these cases as clearly pathological, prolonged, or regressive childhood (preoedipal) symbiosis with the mother.

It might be most fruitful to speculate and investigate this question: Are there inherent factors, so far undetermined, which inexorably lead to a homosexual outcome or are we dealing entirely with an adaptive failure of damaged ego? Why, in one of the cases I shall describe, given the same set of parents, did Mrs. F become homosexual, while her brother is most decidedly heterosexual? The same question arises in the other case; however, the reasons for different outcomes are more apparent.

Miss and Mrs. F

A homosexual relationship existed for 10 years between two sisters-in-law. It was terminated by the hospitalization of Miss F following a severe episode of disorientation; diagnosis: acute schizophrenia.

Mrs. F, in describing her marriage to Miss F's brother, said it had been "for laughs." It seems that the husband is also homosexual. Although this was never explicitly stated, upon separation from his wife, he took up life with another man, with whom he has lived and traveled to this date.

Miss F, the schizophrenic partner, was about 28 years old when the relationship began. Her history includes some highly traumatic material: Mother was permanently hospitalized as a dangerous, assaultive psychotic when Miss F was five years old. The father was a chronic alcoholic. The sister, age nine, and brother, then about seven, were repeatedly removed from and returned to the father's care as his condition continued to deteriorate. They were kept by most unwilling relatives, who both abused and neglected them. Nevertheless, both children succeeded in graduating from high school and in obtaining jobs.

In her middle twenties, Miss F began work as an officer in the New York City Correction Department prison for women. She was a chronically dishevelled, dirty, odiferous person who obviously seldom bathed or changed her clothing. She was most reluctant to be seen without her outer garments in the employees' locker room.

One most notable behavioral feature of Miss F was a tendency to agree with any statement, no matter how absurd; "I guess you're right," she would respond, literally, to a statement that day was night. Her facial expression was bland and blank generally; however, there were, frequently, strange grimacings and inappropriate laughter, which subsided as inexplicably as it began into blandness. Of course, she was regarded as eccentric by her fellows; however, her "calmness" was taken to be the opposite of mental aberration, and there was much shock expressed when she "went off," as will be described below.

Mrs. F was born in Ireland of working class parents. Father was a carpenter; mother was not employed. She, too, had a brother, younger and much adored by her. When she was about eight years old, the family moved to London and thereby Mrs. F began a lifelong fantasy and family romance. Although the family lived in England for only six years, Mrs. F (somewhat jocularly, in response to teasing, but essentially seriously) maintained allegiance to "The Queen." She refused to describe or recognize herself as an American—"you Yanks"—although citizenship had naturally been obtained for her as a minor when the family migrated to the United States. She spoke with a deliberately strong, somewhat forced British accent. Her mother shed all but a trace of accent, the brother speaks typical New Yorkese, while her father retained an Irish brogue. Her speech was full of phrases such as: "at home" (England) and "*we* know our place socially but you Americans have no sense of class or manners," and the like.

Mrs. F was in every observable way the opposite of her sister-in-law. While the latter was gross, heavy, crude, although soft-spoken, filthy, and smelly, Mrs. F was witty, dainty, painfully thin (she suffered from anorexia), always immaculate, and neat. Any narcissism in the choice of these two for each other must have been in fantasy; it surely was not reflected in reality.

The relationship of the two women began before Mrs. F's marriage to Mr. F ("for laughs"). The three bought a very small house together and set up a menage. Shortly after, Mr. F left, and the two women remained. Miss F played the role of husband; she did repairs and various forms of heavy work about the house. Mrs. F played the wife domestically; she cooked, made curtains, etc. Eventually, she, too, came to work at the prison. The relationship was not particularly concealed. Sometimes there would be not-too-veiled spouse-like discussions in the hearing of others, so that no doubt abided even in the most naive observer.

One outstanding feature of the relationship was the apparent control Mrs. F exerted over Miss F. When Miss F would become incoherent (which she did long before her breakdown, responding inappropriately or failing to complete sentences in reporting incidents), Mrs. F would bring her up short with "Stop that nonsense!" This treatment was effective. Miss F would, for the nonce, stop the nonsense.

Miss F's schizophrenic breakdown occurred when the two were on vacation in the Caribbean. She somehow broke away from her mentor and returned to New York alone before Mrs F could find her. She was now disoriented. She came to the home of a fellow employee for whom she had always expressed great dislike and implored her to be allowed to remain in her home as she was afraid of Mrs. F. She wanted to be hidden, but at the same time, returned to work one week before the expiration of her vacation. Meanwhile, Mrs. F had returned, but Miss F refused to stay with her. Just where she lived during the next three weeks remains unknown.

During this period, Miss F's speech was incoherent. Her grimacing became greatly exaggerated; she paced back and forth, walking to and from nowhere. She was protected from her supervisors by the inmates of the prison, who recognized her condition and were sympathetic, supervising themselves so that she would not be found out. Of course, even though the supervisors were reluctant to act, the fact of Miss F's condition finally had to be faced. Her brother was summoned, and she was removed to a city hospital psychiatric ward, from which she was committed to a state hospital. She remained there for eight years, during which her "privileges" were increased. Today she is employed as a clerk. Her physical appearance has not changed; she is still dirty. Her manner is similar to that preceding her breakdown in the past.

Mrs. F was quite distraught at Miss F's commitment. She insisted that she could have prevented it if only Miss F hadn't gotten away from her. She expressed utter contempt and loathing for the psychiatric staff at the hospital; she said she had been told that Miss F would never be released into her custody or even with any association with her.

With Miss F gone from the picture, Mrs. F became the queen bee of a hive of females. There were four followers of her orders. Three of these women had never married; the fourth was a divorcee. There were, from time to time, temporary additions to the bee-hive.

As to her homosexuality, Mrs. F's fantasy life—British and wellborn—may have gotten in the way of normal development. The fact of the lack of authority on the part of the father stands out as a feature of her childhood (Pasche, in Gillespie, 1964). The impression is that of a man browbeaten and not participating in the raising of the brother and sister or in important family decisions. He did take a firm stand on the family following him to America; he cut off funds. He was not forgiven. For the most part, he played the part of a leprechaun in the home—his "cute" sayings were quoted but he was not taken too seriously. Mrs. F did identify strongly with her mother—a phallic type, overbearing and masterly—although the two quarreled bitterly at times.

The case of the sister-in-law, Miss F, exhibits a plethora of childhood trauma and symptoms. Among the symptoms was grossly distorted body image as evidenced by an extreme masculinity and by physical filthiness. Her ego seemed structurally disintegrated; no evidence of repression (she seemed to expect that all would accept her role as a man). Her most evident defense was that of denial. Functions of integration and synthesis were severely impaired. At her best she was not capable of coherent thinking; ideas did not match or combine in her thinking. During her acute episode, she was pitifully hunting for "the clue," which she said was a map she had somehow misplaced.

Miss CC

The initials CC were not chosen at random, nor do they represent the true name or pseudonym of the second case. CC in this case stands for "Classic Case," for this woman's evolution into overt homosexuality had about it so many of the elements discussed in the literature and an almost classic tragic inevitability. CC is in her early fifties, of average build and looks. She is a successful college instructor in biology. She furnished the following data for this paper, for the most part. Some of the information is based on the writer's long acquaintance with CC.

When she was born, the second of two daughters, her father wept because he had so longed for a son. To her recollection, this story was repeatedly told to her, at least as early as she could comprehend its meaning, by family friends and by her parents. This factor—"the preference of . . . sex by parents" is mentioned by Weiss (in Socarides, 1962).

The parents, people of high intellect and education, were not happy together or well suited; probably at a later time in history they would have been divorced. To exacerbate the father's disappointment, there had been an abortion two years after the birth of the first daughter, which he had opposed, and which he became convinced had disposed of the desired boy child. One week before his sudden death, CC, then in her late twenties, heard him talking to a tradesman. He was still bemoaning his lack of sons. In relating this incident, she confessed to a lingering sense of guilt at having so saddened her father's life.

Another facet was the dominance of the mother in the home. The father's chosen business took him out of town for weeks at a time. During the short intervals when he was at home, his role as father was mainly confined to inquiring as to school progress and the like. CC felt no conscious filial attachment to father and thought that both parents preferred her very pretty sister. However, she did woo both.

CC was a very gifted child and progressed very rapidly through grade school. Her precocity was enhanced by maternal instruction in reading at age four and continued interest in her reading. She was ready to enter college at age 15. She was athletic, strong, and healthy, in contrast to an ailing delicate sister. This, combined with parental endogenous needs and confusions, led to her being treated in a manner more suitable to an adult or much older child. Much was expected of her, and she was encouraged in a precocious independence (precocious ego development). However, her maturation and development were quite uneven, in line with situations described by Anna Freud (1963). Thus, she was enuretic until age eight, sometimes consciously and vindictively wetting the bed after joining her sleeping sister, sometimes to arouse her mother's anger. Although intellectually advanced, it was obvious by the time she reached adolescence that she was socially quite far behind. She was inordinately shy and more and more alienated from her coevals as they advanced to sexual maturity. There was no overt autoeroticism after age four. She is a very heavily addicted smoker.

Gender Identity

In reviewing the genesis of CC's homosexuality, it becomes evident that she "never had a chance." Father assured her repeatedly of the unworthiness of her being a girl. He made no comments about her clothing or appearance, while continuing to praise the beauty of the older daughter. When CC, at adolescence, began to affect masculine dress as far as such dress would be tolerated in school, father bought her presents of men's pajamas! The mother, usually a very forceful woman, raised only feeble objections to CC's mannerisms and garb. The objections were couched in sarcastic terms, and the response was usually angry silence. Meanwhile, CC was ambivalent about the response of others to her appearance; she both welcomed and dreaded the attention elicited. As to oedipal resolution, there could be none with an ephemeral, rejecting father. Her wooing of her father by means of her talents only served to confirm her masculine strivings.

Early Heterosexual Experiences

CC's parents were exceedingly intimate with another family. There were five considerably older children than CC. She was much petted in their home, where she spent considerable time. The son closest in age was her adored companion from the time she was four and he ten until his serious attachment, during CC's adolescence, to the girl he eventually married. CC recalls that this boy used to masturbate her occasionally during "hide and seek" games in closets and corners when she was about five or six years old, and that the experience was pleasurable. Her mother "did not hear" her proud report of these doings. The eldest son in this family, a young man well in his twenties, frequently grabbed at her breasts as they began to develop, about the time she was ten or eleven. She greatly resented this and his exhibiting his genitals to her. The experience was felt as a humiliating assault on her person and part of the inferior position of being a girl. She deferred learning the mechanics of sexual intercourse until fourteen; then she reacted with excitement, seeing herself in the male posture. Simone de Beauvoir describes in *The Second Sex* the resentment of females in their biological, passive role.

Homosexual Choice

CC "consciously chose" homosexuality at about age 14. During the previous year, there had been a last desperate effort at heterosexuality and femininity of dress and demeanor. The effort failed; there was poor response from males, as the damage had already been done; the adored "brother" mentioned above had made his choice. She dropped out of competition with both mother and sister, as described by Freud (1920). As if to prove her feelings were valid, she almost immediately entered into a relationship with a much older married woman. For the first time, she felt attractive, and this feeling was certainly confirmed by her continued success as a homosexual. CC was attracted only to seemingly heterosexual women, usually mothers. This is in line with the "Resonance Identification" with "vaginally aroused women" mentioned by Socarides (1962). All her life, CC has felt a residue of heterosexual feelings—she describes herself humorously as a "repressed heterosexual"—but a permanent homosexual relationship and her homosexual pathology were too strong for her even to attempt experimentally to have sexual experiences with men.

Thoughts and Conclusions

The centricity of the role of the father and other male figures in the etiology of female homosexuality has been stressed in this paper.

It is a point somewhat neglected in the literature on the subject, just as the role of the father is underemphasized in the etiology of other pathology. Can it be that most workers and writers are male? Or are females educated and conditioned by males, and thus find it more self-syntonic to blame "mother" than to blame "father" (themselves) for the psychic ills of their patients? We are not here concerned with righting the social situation of women, but rather concerned with a search for truth. Of course, no one can doubt the preeminence of the mother; her role is the sine qua non of human development, normal or pathological. But it is time to draw father out of the closet. He is at least as important in the oedipal situation of both girls and boys as the mother; no successful resolution can occur if father is absent, indifferent, or rejecting.

In the case of Mrs. F, the part played by the father was unauthoritative. All important family decisions, especially the move to England and the choice of religion, were made by the mother, sometimes against his wishes. (He remained a Catholic; of course, the rest became Anglican, so very British were they.) His position was peripheral.

Mrs. F's "femininity" on the surface was never in doubt. Her *femaleness* never developed beyond marrying an apparently homosexual Mr. F for "laughs." Of course, in a strange way, the marriage may have been an attempt at restitution of heterosexuality.

The schizophrenic Miss F was so ravaged by such serious childhood trauma that her case really deserves separate exposition. The role of her father can be assessed in terms of his alcoholism, brutality, and neglect of the child before and after the hospitalization and absence of the mother. Miss F's ego development can be assumed to have been fatally inhibited during the first months and years of life with a disorientated psychotic mother. Whatever autonomous development occurred was damaged beyond repair by subsequent psychic and physical abuse. Defenses were scarcely evident. She had recourse only to withdrawal from the battle. "I guess you're right."

As for CC, father clearly can be assessed as a most causative element in her homosexual outcome, with a certain concurrence by the mother. His outspoken disappointment in her sex, his denial of her femininity, his open admiration and acceptance of the other daughter, his encouragement of boyish activities, while the mother, caught in an unhappy marriage, stood dreamily by, were mentioned in the case presentation. (A word must be added as to sibling difficulties—hopeless competition for paternal love and approval—as an important element.) Filial obedience demanded that CC play the role of the male. Unresolved oedipal problems forbade male (incestuous) sex partners. Other crucial male figures, the two quasi brothers, were important factors as well. The younger brother aroused CC's childish heterosexual feelings, but married another girl. Her "conscious" decision as to homosexuality followed almost immediately after his engagement. The other, older brother, a grown man, both aroused her and shamed her by his mauling. His exhibiting his mature genitalia was, to her, the "penis shock" mentioned by Fenichel (1945). An interesting sidelight is the fact that this brother made the same approaches to CC's sister, who, probably because of greater ego strength, did not appear to have been traumatized, sexually at least.

Therapy

It is generally agreed that homosexuals whose aberration is oedipally based are more treatable than those with very early fixation or far-reaching regression to infantile sexuality. The same is true for oscillating bisexuals, as compared with the overt homosexuals.

Most writers treat guardedly the subjects of prognosis and treatment in homosexuality. Wiedeman (1962) quotes Freud, Fenichel, and others who hold out little hope for "cure" through psychoanalysis, nor do they mention *any* approach with optimism. Wiedeman also quotes Eissler's aim (p. 404) as that of making the perverse symptom ego-alien, and that does seem a good aim. How can it be done? Socarides (1962) quotes Edoardo Weiss: "Success in therapeutically awakening heterosexual desires in an overt homosexual woman depends on many factors: on her motivation to experience heterosexual feelings, on her age, on her commitment to homosexual enjoyment, on her constitutional disposition, on the flexibility of her ego, and on the strength of her resistance against the repressed or eluded oedipus complex" (p. 588).

Few of these caveats appear to trouble Bergler (1957): "He [the homosexual] is *curable.*" In his book, he purports to give verbatim reports of sessions with his homosexual patients. These sessions can be compared with a prolonged bullfight, Bergler being a clever, sarcastic, and adroit matador who cannot help winning over and demolishing the stubborn, wrong-headed animal, who has only his poor instincts and primitive defenses. He reports such startling success that it is to be wondered why this technique cannot be applied universally to all disturbances of the human psyche. Therapists will be surprised to learn of the therapeutic value of irony, wit, logic, etc.

As our society is evolving, homosexuality, as well as "free" heterosexuality and other forms of sexual expression, are seemingly being skinned of their coatings of guilt and shame. At this writing, I have on my desk some literature that I requested from the Mattachine Society of New York, an organization of homosexuals whose avowed aim is to make the homosexual "proud" of his sexual orientation. Twice weekly an FM radio station quite popular with young people broadcasts a program called "Gay Pride," which has a program more militant than that of the Mattachine Society. If these aims succeed, if guilt is no longer a reliable ally,* what will be the approach of future therapists?

---

*Guilt never was a reliable ally. If the thrust forward in development is absent then we *have no* ally; how to find that thrust forward remains the therapeutic task.

References

Bergler, E. (1957). *Homosexuality: Disease or way of life?* New York: Hill and Wang.

Fenichel, O. (1945). *The psychoanalytic theory of neurosis.* New York: W.W. Norton.

Freud, A. (1963). *The concept of developmental lines.* London: P.S.C.

Freud, S. (1905). *Three essays on the theory of sexuality.* New York: Avon.

Freud, S. (1920). *The psychogenesis of a case of homosexuality in a woman.* New York: Collier.

Gillespie, W. H. (1964). Symposium on homosexuality. *Journal of International Psychoanalysis, 45,* 2.

Jacobson, E. (1964). *The self and the object world.* New York: International Universities Press.

Socarides, C. W. (1962). Theoretical and clinical aspects of overt female homosexuality. *Journal of the American Psychoanalytic Association, 10,* 3.

Wiedeman, G. H. (1962). Survey of psychoanalytic literature on overt male homosexuality. *Journal of the American Psychoanalytic Association, 10,* 2.

Object Relations Insights Concerning the Female as Artist

Susan Kavaler-Adler, Ph.D.

Do women have gender-specific patterns related to their use of the creative process for artistic self expression? There seem to be some aspects of creative psychology that can be looked at particularly in relation to women, and intrapsychic object relations will be the focus of this paper's explorations. The role of the female's father will be highlighted in relation to the tendency toward creative addiction in those women who seek to create from within their interior worlds. The poet Emily Dickinson will be examined, along with a current-day psychotherapy patient, to illustrate the psychodynamics of those engaged in artistic creativity. A developmental view of unconscious fantasy and its object relations aspects will be presented.

An Extreme Case

Emily Dickinson was ready-made to become a romantic myth in the nineteenth century. Yet even today, the myth surrounding her withdrawal into seclusion to create a brilliant form of subjective poetry has far from diminished. In fact, the romantic aura of her myth has been enhanced as biographers and literary critics have dubbed Dickinson the most profound, provocative, and, overall, the greatest American poet. This is quite significant in that Emily Dickinson was a woman, and very little has been written about the drive or urge to create in women, while much has been written about creativity though the study of male artists, for example, Hemingway, Lawrence, Shakespeare, Fitzgerald. Biographers have studied individual women artists and writers, but comparisons among such women have been relatively rare. (This study, and its full length counterpart in Kavaler-Adler's *The Compulsion to Create,* in press, are attempts to redress this imbalance.)

For many creative persons, there can be an irresistible pull inward, away from external objects and toward seclusion. This tendency to turn into one's self is generally a limited phenomenon. It is felt as an internal cry to return to a deep state of concentration from which the inner life is free to flow forth, onto canvas or paper. The craving for this state can be so intense that when deprived of it, the artist may feel blocked, suffocated, clogged up, or affectively starved—in the way that a drug addict might feel when deprived of drugs. This viscerally felt need for withdrawal generally culminates in a period of intense imaginative cognition, which has its own climax and denouement. Following such periods, a sense of deep fulfillment can enable the creative artist to reconnect with the outside world and its external objects.

A study of Emily Dickinson's life reveals a withdrawal that goes significantly beyond that of most artists. Withdrawing permanently from the world outside her family home, she created a state of self-captivity within her own seclusion (see Cody, 1971; Wolff, 1985; Sewall, 1980).

Emily Dickinson withdrew increasingly from the world after one year attending Mount Holyoke College. Although actively involved with friendships (mainly female) and classroom studies during her high school days at Amherst Academy, she was quick to withdraw from a college that kept her in residence away from her family home, and particularly away from her father. One of Dickinson's biographers, and a Dickinson scholar, Richard Sewall, emphasizes the role that her father played in enticing her to leave college and to reside once more within the walls of his patriarchal family home. Emily Dickinson's father dominated both her external and internal worlds, but his role in dominating her internal world and the creative world that emanated from within this interior female space can only have been intensified and exacerbated by her increasing withdrawal from the world that followed. Emily not only returned home to live after one year of college, but she began to withdraw from all social engagements, so that by the time she was 30 she never went beyond her family home's garden. Sometimes, she would withdraw even further and fail to come out of her bedroom. When her brother Austin's dear friend and lover, Mabel Todd Lewis, would visit and play the piano, Emily would stay hidden upstairs listening and would convey her thanks for the concert by having a maid carry a tray downstairs with a glass of wine or a flower on it.

Renunciation and Seclusion

Renunciation—is a piercing Virtue—
The letting go
A Presence—for an Expectation
Not now—
The putting out of Eyes—
Just Sunrise—
Lest Day—
Day's Great Progenitor—
Outvie

Complete Poems, #745

Seclusion was defended by Dickinson as a mode of renunciation necessary for a true commitment to creative work. Yet unconscious fantasies revealed in her work indicate that this reason for seclusion was mere rationalization. Her continuing choice to stay at home, and particularly to withdraw from relations with men, even when later in life she was asked to be the wife of a man she loved and adored (Judge Otis P. Lord), can be seen to express deep unconscious fears and wishes. Connecting her ability to create with isolation from others can be seen to reflect three developmental levels of psychic fantasy: the reunion, the internal king, and the spiritual bride.

The Reunion Fantasy

Because I could not stop for Death—
He kindly stopped for me—
The Carriage held but just Ourselves—

And Immortality.

Complete Poems, #712

Emily Dickinson's internal world was dominated by a masculine presence. This presence appeared as a god-demon, who might be seen as an archaic father with whom she merged, married, engaged in battle, and with whom she ultimately identified. There are many developmental levels represented in her psychic fantasy life, as it emerged in her poetic work, but the most primary level appears to be that of a symbiotic reunion or remerger. In the above poem, the reunion is with a masculinized figure of death, who comes to take her to his land of "immortality." Either rebirth or abandonment into a void awaits her. The poem is left equivocal. Yet, the dominance of the masculine figure is evident, as is the dominance of fate, and it follows a trend of all Dickinson's poems in this regard.

Throughout Dickinson's poetry, she appears engaged in a battle with a demonic god who abandons and betrays her (Kavaler, 1991; Wolff, 1986). She is enmeshed with this god-demon in such a way that the battle resembles an oppositional symbiosis of preoedipal intensity. Yet, this god-demon can also appear as a demon lover, an eroticized figure in which primitive idealization is compounded by oedipal-stage erotic yearnings. In a pathological twist, seemingly due to the arrested nature of Dickinson's schizoid character, her oedipal father is not an erotic figure of human proportions, but an archaic god of superhuman proportions who becomes eroticized. Her creative passion seems to emerge continuously from the conflictual love and hate that she holds toward this form of a demon-lover father figure. Yet, just as her father-god turns demonic, so he is apt to turn into the persona of death. This trend of transformation is one followed by many preoedipally arrested female artists, with examples seen in the life and work of Sylvia Plath (Kavaler, 1985, 1986), Diane Arbus (Kavaler, 1988), and Ann Sexton (Kavaler, 1989). It is a trend that can often lead to suicide, but in Emily Dickinson's case it seems to have led to an increasing withdrawal from the world, accompanied by fantasies of remerger with a preoedipal object father through death. Such a reunion fantasy is a macabre form of the general borderline reunion fantasies described by Masterson (1972, 1981). Yet, the theme of wishes for symbiotic union, exclusive of the rest of the world, remains prominent.

Related to such an internal world reunion fantasy is the narcissistic cocoon fantasy described by Modell (1975). Such fantasy can be seen explicitly in the work of Sylvia Plath, who writes of folding her children back inside of her to curl into herself just before she suicides (Plath, 1961):

> Each dead child coiled, a white serpent,
> One at each little
>
> Pitcher of milk, now empty.
> She has folded
>
> Them back into her body as petals
> Of a rose close when the garden
>
> Stiffens and odours bleed
> From the sweet, deep throats of the night flower.
>
> "Edge," *Ariel*, p. 84

In Emily Dickinson such a cocoon fantasy is not explicit, but is implied by her enactment of such a fantasy through her withdrawal from the world. The fantasy of withdrawal into rebirth through death, or into a secure environment from which one can be reborn into a better world, is discussed by Winnicott (1965) and Guntrip (1976), when they describe the phenomenology of the schizoid preoedipal character. Modell (1975, 1976), however, emphasizes the withdrawal into the cocoon itself as being a goal, the goal of mergence with a primary archaic other that is delusionally believed to make one self-sufficient in respect to external objects. For the creative schizoid personality, the enactment or fantasy of withdrawal into one's own cocoon may actually be linked with cure, not just with survival. To withdraw and to create from one's inner self—an inner self split off and cut off from the false self that encounters the world—then becomes the wished for cure. The fantasy cure involves a wished-for self-other reparation, but it requires renunciation of relations with the world, and the relations most renounced by schizoid women, such as Dickinson, are with men. Relations with men become a threat to the solitary womb of creative activity, in which the internal father-god-demon is sought for symbiotic reunion. Perhaps such renunciation in schizoid women is not unique. Perhaps it applies more generally to all women, particularly creative women, with a continuum stretching off from the schizoid personality extreme.

The Internal King Fantasy

I have a King, who does not speak
So—wondering—thro' the hours meek
I trudge the day away—
Half glad when it is night, and sleep,
If, haply, thr' a dream, to peep
In parlors, shut by day.

And if I do—when morning comes—
It is as if a hundred drums
Did round my pillow roll,
And shouts fill all my childish sky,
And Bells keep saying "Victory"
From steeples in my soul!

Complete Poems, #103

The above poem is Dickinson's attempt to describe her internal dream king, the masculine force and object that arose to consciousness through her dreams. The poet tells us that she is elated when her internal king appears to her through a dream at night. She becomes expansive with a victorious ecstasy and feels the phallic-like pride of "steeples in my soul!" The latter lines of the poem, not reported here, speak of how deflated and bereft she becomes when she fails to fortify herself through contact with her internal king through the dark shades of dreams at night.

This poetic statement of Dickinson's seems to reflect her intense yearning for identification with an incorporated father, who again appears with omnipotent god-like dimensions, as "king." On the days when she experienced her dream king rising within her, she would feel fertile with creative expression. On the days when he failed to come—as Emily Bronte's male muse failed to appear (see Gerin, 1971; Hatfield, 1941)—Dickinson would feel depleted of her creative urge, force, and desire. She would suffer an absence of symbolic fecundity. Such association between the conscious encounter of her internal male object and the vitality of her creative capacities has led one biographer (Ward, 1961) to speculate that Dickinson's creative life was dominated by the Jungian masculine archetype, the animus. Cody (1971), from a more Freudian perspective, proposes that Dickinson's dream king was a representation of her internal father, with whom she had come to identify as a way to promote the salient aspect of herself that emerged within her creativity. Either view links the poet's ability to manifest her creative capacities with a masculine component of her personality that was unintegrated into her larger self structure, thus resulting in its tentative and temporary appearance.

Monick (1929), another Jungian, has spoken of a more general appearance of a phallic force in women that makes Dickinson's experience representative of the many. He writes:

> What place, then, does phallus-animus have in the creative life of women without recourse to a man or masculine image on whom she can project her phallic qualities?
>
> Phallos can be a guide to a woman as he is to a man. His stirring, metaphorically, lets a woman know that creative action is on the horizon. . . . The stirring of phallos in a man shows his impending readiness to sow seed; in a woman, the positive aspect of animus manifests in impulses to establish herself creatively in the world. (p. 123)

Another explanation of Dickinson's phallic arousal promoting creative arousal could be the combining of incestuous desires toward the father from the oedipal stage with preoedipal cravings for symbiotic merger, following preoedipal developmental arrest due to inadequate separation from a severely schizoid mother (see Wolff, 1985). Such a combination would promote an excessively masculine identity, particularly in light of an inadequate feminine identification contributing to a depletion of the more innate feminine aspects of the self.

As paternal incorporation prompts varying levels of phallic identification, we see accompanying erotic yearnings toward the father-god-king. The poem of the dream king speaks of the desire to "peep in parlors, shut by day." The poet seems to be telling her readers that she has a secret rendezvous in the dark, which implies an incestuous rendezvous with her paternal dream king. In another poem, such speculation is confirmed, as Dickinson writes:

> What need of Day—/To those whose Dark—hath so—surpassing Sun—/It deem it be—Continually—/At the Meridian?
>
> *Complete Poems*, #611

If we understand "Sun" to mean father, as is customary in Dickinson's use of symbolism (Cody, 1971, p. 434), we see the poet speaking of seeking her father in the darkness, in the secret silence of the night. This takes on added meaning when Dickinson's poetry also transmits the message that fantasy is preferable to reality (Cody, 1971, p. 434), in that she can use fantasy to be rich in creative expression. Not only does she seek her father in the night, but she seeks her incestuous night union with him as the source of her creative life, as dreams promote fantasy.

The Spiritual Bride Fantasy

McNeil (1986), in her study of Dickinson, writes: "Edward seems to have selected Emily to stay with him, rather the way Emerson chose his clever daughter, Evelyn Tucker" (p. 92). From this assumption concerning Edward Dickinson's motives in keeping his daughter at home with him, McNeil goes on to link such paternal behavior with Emily's reactions to it. She mentions Emily Dickinson's portrayal of the "spiritual bride," a role she clearly distinguishes from the worldly wife who must rise, or possibly bend, to meet her husband's "requirements" (*Complete Poems*, #732). From her poetry, it can easily be seen that Emily Dickinson identified herself as a "spiritual bride," and women such as her mother with the indentured wife who must live to fulfill her husband's desires:

> She rose to His Requirement—dropt
> The Playthings of Her Life
> to take the honorable Work
> Of Woman, and of Wife—
>
> *Complete Poems*, #732

To be the "spiritual bride" was to escape the role of wife, but the secret of union that she held as such a bride was an incestuous union with her father. The oedipal wish to marry her father could only be consummated in the darkness of the night through the mist of dreams, fantasy, and poetry. Psychic incest would therefore haunt the poet from within, even as she evaded all men and marriages by day. The spiritual bride is married through the soul rather than through the body, but Dickinson wrote of the soul that reached its "white heat": "Dare you see a Soul at the White Heat?" (*Complete Poems,* #365). There was a fire within her that was part of her mystery, and she never could fully explain it. It was at the crescendo of such "white heat" that she often wrote poetry, inspired by the same form of compulsion as Sylvia Plath, who bled out her last days *Ariel* poems in a manic frenzy at 5:00 a.m. Dickinson both loved and hated the intensity, as she loved and hated her father-god. But even as she was imprisoned by it, she also created from it, and ultimately she turned down marriage with a man she loved (Judge Otis T. Lord) in order to continue it. There seems to be far more eroticism in Dickinson's spiritual "white heat" than the poet could imagine in proposed sexual union. Sexual union could threaten a loss of self or identity, while this spiritual bride union of the soul promoted an identity through the verbal communications of poetry.

The Internal Father and Addictive Tendencies in Creative Women

The three constellations of psychic fantasies just discussed represent three somewhat overlapping levels of development. The reunion fantasy stems from the early symbiotic phases of preoedipal development. The internal king fantasy stems from practicing-stage phallic dispositions. The spiritual bride fantasy stems from oedipal stage yearnings. Yet all overlap through their emphasis on tantalizing attraction to the father figure in female development. Even the preoedipal yearnings have been transferred to the father, who overlaps with the primary mothering object in his archaic form. Although Cody (1971) emphasizes the homosexual yearnings in Dickinson, resulting from frustrated desires for the preoedipal mother, Dickinson's poetry continuously featured the father as the symbolized object of love and hate.

Perhaps Dickinson's withdrawal from the world was an enactment of her mother's schizoid mode of being, but her internal world, as presented to us in her poetry, had the father as dominating any representational object form. Perhaps the father was several degrees less merged with the poet than was her mother, and thus his form could take on more vivid differentiation within the poet's internal world. Also, it appears that the poet's mental merger between her mother and father made any archaic maternal form take on a masculinized veneer. Yet, even more importantly, the father would be the eroticized love object at the oedipal stage for a woman, and his dominance as such a love object may contribute to an overshadowing of the maternal form by the paternal form within the internal world. If this is true for a preoedipal woman, such as Dickinson, it would be even more true for higher level women, women without developmental arrests who have triadic oedipal-stage constellations.

Insofar as the father is then associated with the creative urge in artistic women such as Dickinson, the father's role in psychic fantasies will affect many aspects of a woman's creative life. For Dickinson, the yearning for the father promoted a retreat into seclusion that was rationalized as a necessary condition for creative work. Perhaps the creative work was felt to be the mode of union with the father on all three developmental levels represented by psychic fantasies. The seeking of seclusion would then be determined by object yearnings toward an internal object, the father of the internal world. Can we see such behavior in other women? Can we see such behavior in higher level creative women, even if not so extreme?

Women in General

Years of clinical work with women who have sought help through psychotherapy and psychoanalysis suggest that a wide range of women may exhibit the kind of seclusive tendencies in relation to the exercise of their creative potentials that in Emily Dickinson were so profound. Whether these women had developed an artistic talent from childhood, or whether they had only discovered such a talent following a course of psychotherapy in which an individuated identity first began to bloom—across a continuum of developmental levels and diagnostic groups—such women all seem to show a belief that they could not create unless they sequestered their creative activities in a private world that particularly excluded men. On the other hand, these women would become obsessed with men at times, at the expense of any continuing development of their creative talents. When excluding men from their lives, they would exhibit the defensive psychodynamics of creative compulsion or addiction. When obsessed with men, to the exclusion of their creative work, they would exhibit the symptoms of creative blocks.

To illustrate this thesis, I will present the case of one female analysand who stands in contrast to Emily Dickinson in having reached the oedipal stage of development through treatment (despite an initial preoedipal character pattern).

The Case of Ms. T

Ms. T entered psychotherapy (later to become psychoanalysis) at a time when her life was in chaos. She had just begun to work and live independently, after leaving her mother's home. She had not yet found a way to use her academic master's degree, which she had obtained at an out-of-town university, and she was working at a job that was minimal in pay and which was below her level of intellectual ability and educated competence. In addition, the job was totally unsuited to her interests, since it required basic mathematical computations, when she had skills and interests in the arts and in the social sciences. Besides this inappropriate job situation, Ms. T was indiscriminately dating men with whom she had little or nothing in common. She would pick up these men in bars or nightclubs, would generally spend the night with them, and would then assume that they would treat her like a girlfriend and form a commitment, when this was never the case in reality. She would be shocked and full of despair and anguish when she was dropped by these men, but she would continue to sleep with and date such men in an addictive way without learning from any of her disappointing experiences.

At one point, Ms. T found a man who was interested in becoming engaged to her. Despite numerous disappointments with his inability to share any of her interests, values, or hopes for the future, she persisted in fantasies of being his wife, until her fiancé dropped her to appease his family, who threatened to disown him for marrying a woman from a different ethnic group.

Over the years, in both psychotherapeutic and psychoanalytic treatment, Ms. T got in touch with memories of painful losses in relation to her parents' divorce when she was 15, and her father's abandonment of her and her family. As she discovered her rage at the men she dated in the present, she would be brought back to the rage at her abandoning father and would experience more and more the anguished mourning for the father of her early childhood, to whom she had been so attached. She also experienced rage toward the mother of her teenage years, whom formerly she had seen merely as her father's victim. She began to remember vividly her mother's contempt toward her, and dismissal of her, at a time when her mother escaped from her own pain into a pattern of promiscuous dating. Ms. T's mother would flaunt her heterosexual escapades in front of her isolated teenage daughter, who was being mocked by girls at school and ignored by the teenage boys. Yet, her mother was the only parent Ms. T had left, and it wasn't until years later in psychotherapy that she could face how abandoned and abused she had felt by the mother whom she had idealized, victimized, and identified with within her own mind.

Like Emily Dickinson, Ms. T harbored deep wishes toward both her parents that had become consolidated around intrapsychic fantasies of reunion with an idealized father figure. Each fling with a man had been her attempt at receiving eroticized nurturance from a lost father who had become idealized to defend against tremendous rage and agonizing grief. Only by remembering her real father and by facing her feelings toward him, while internalizing him as he actually was, could she let go of her addictive patterns of indiscriminate involvement with men. As she did so, she became free to focus on aspects of her life that were separate from men. She got a job that was more appropriate to her education, interest, and skills. She was able to leave that job, too, when she was not being treated well, and get a job that was even more appropriate to her skills and interests. Also, she began to date more appropriate men, and even had a sustained and related involvement with a man who shared her work interests.

Then, at the time when this relationship was brought to an end, Ms. T began to explore new areas of self-development within creative activities. She thought about returning to childhood interests in music and dance. However, she ultimately discovered that her main creative interest and talent lay in writing. As she opened to this awareness, she was able to concentrate on her own creative work as she had never done before. This was an extreme contrast from the days of her love addiction enactment with men, when she could not be alone at all and would compulsively call men with whom she sought her fantasy reunion with father.

In treatment she had learned how to mourn by mourning with the analyst. First she mourned for each of the lost men in her life, and then ultimately, and also interactively, for her father himself. Now, she could mourn while alone, listening to recordings of romantic music to stimulate her memories and longings into full awareness. Mourning became an introduction to creative work, as well as an intricate part of it. She would listen to music, cry, remember, and then sit down to express herself in creative writing. She began to consult other writers about technique and form, and used her acquired knowledge to discipline her writing efforts. Yet, her mode of concentration was always induced by contracting fantasies and memories of her father and the father-figure male displacements to whom she had varying forms of attachment to now. Unlike Emily Dickinson, Ms. T had a core feminine self developed from her early years, so she did not substitute a paternal-male identification for a feminine one. Still, her writing became both feminine and phallic as she not only birthed it and brought it forth into the world, but also began to aggressively promote herself as a writer.

Surprisingly for a former love addict, as Ms. T moved forward with such creative development, she moved away from men. She resisted showing her work to men who inquired about it. She stopped all formal dating, although she had not long before explored many new avenues to meeting men. She developed an infection that prevented her from having sex for a period of time, and she believed that her body was "saving" her from giving herself away to men so that she could continue her creative work. She often wondered if this infection was psychologically based, and although she cursed her fate, she repeatedly and almost incessantly remarked that her body was protecting her from sabotaging her newfound development, in particular, her creative development. Any encounters that she did have with men at this time, she would use in the service of her mourning and writing. If touched by a man at this time, rather than have sex with him, she would wed him through fantasy interconnected with paternal memories, through the format of her expressive writing.

Ms. T was relieved that as her analyst, I could understand that she was developing herself by her seclusion from men at this time. She was deeply touched by my empathic comprehension of her wish to forsake men, for a while at least, so that she could write. She expressed much anger at a former male therapist who had seen her writing as a defensive avoidance of dating men. It was quite a while until she could discuss with me the possibility that there might be a defensive aspect to her way of using her writing at that time, and that she was defending against a fear that emotional involvement with men might either dry up her reservoir of reunion memories with men, so that she would have no material to write, or would seriously disable her abilities to concentrate while she attempted to write.

With Emily Dickinson in mind, certain hypotheses about Ms. T's intrapsychic dynamics during this latter period might be put forth. The main hypothesis is that Ms. T, like Dickinson, looked to her creative writing as a modality for experiencing an intrapsychic reunion with her father and the derivative male father figures that accompanied her father's image within her internal world. To be alone then becomes possible, as being alone actually means being alone with her remembered father, and emotionally wedding him, now as a spiritual bride, through creative work and its complementary mourning process. By affectively marrying her father, or father-mother, through her creative work, Ms. T found a route to intrapsychically internalizing her mournfully remembered father figures, so that more and more her internalizations allowed her to not feel isolated when alone. As her internal world became rich with her father and his more loving relations with her, Ms. T began to feel full of creative resources when alone. This felt healing, and such self-reparation reinforced an intrapsychic fantasy of healthy narcissistic self-sufficiency, although the defensive aspects of this self-sufficiency became apparent as Ms. T acted out a fear that to be with a man in her current life would totally destroy her newfound independence.

Was Ms. T keeping all new men out to preserve an incestuously exciting relationship with her father as well as with the past men in her life who had in many ways served as father figures? Was she preserving an early reunion with mother, which had now been transformed into a heterosexual union with her father, as her father was mourned and more securely became her dominant love object? Was she merely protecting a precarious state of independence, a state in which she believed that her ability to concentrate, and thus to rendezvous with her internal objects, would be threatened by external relations, especially relations with men, which were reminiscent of past obsessions? All these questions suggest hypotheses about women in general that might follow from this example of Ms. T.

Yet, what remains most striking is the basic choice that this woman made to safeguard her creative capacities: to seclude herself from romantic relations with men. Such a choice is particularly intriguing in this case because this woman who moved toward excluding men in the symptomatic mode of creative addiction was formerly a love addict, or, in Ms. T's own words, a "male addict." Although Ms. T is moving toward an integration of her romance with men and her romance with her internal men within the "transitional world" of the creative process, the route toward such integration appears to have a distinct stage of heterosexual withdrawal that mirror the lifelong seclusion of the more schizoid Emily Dickinson.

Sociological Factors

The movie "My Brilliant Career" is based on the autobiographical novel of an Australian woman. This story displays a uniquely female conflict, the conflict of marriage versus career, with the heroine ultimately deciding that they are mutually exclusive. After years of desiring a man, the heroine refuses two offers of marriage from her chosen man, and her ultimate refusal is couched in the pretext that marriage would not allow her to write. From what we see of this heroine as a novelist, it appears that she may have published only her one autobiographical tale and no other creative works. Might she perhaps have written, developed, and published more if she had married her man? What made her think that she would not be free to write if she married? Was she afraid she would lose inspiration if she was fulfilled in her erotic desires and joined to a man? Are there real sociological conditions that have made, or still make, marriage seem a threat to female creativity?

The Feminists' View of Emily Dickinson

The feminist literary critics Gilbert and Gubar (1979) maintain that Emily Dickinson's choice to renounce the world, and particularly the world of marriage and men, was a conscious choice that provided the only avenue to self-expression for a woman living within patriarchal Victorian society. Rich (1979), another feminist literary critic (and poet), even more explicitly asserted that Dickinson did what she wanted to do, in the only way she could, in a world where marriage precluded female creativity. These critics totally disregard the intrapsychic and developmental arrest factors that seem to have compelled Dickinson toward such renunciation. Their belief that Dickinson freely chose to reject marriage since marriage made a woman rise "to his requirement" (Gilbert & Gubar, 1979, p. 588) overlooks Dickinson's precarious schizoid state, which made relationships threaten her with self loss. Further, such feminist critics overlook the poet's own reaction to the life she led, shut away from others, with poetry as the only source of spontaneous life that she knew. Wolff (1986), in her extensive and scholarly biography of Dickinson, tells us that at the end of her life the poet wrote poetry that expressed her despair. Wolff (1985) writes that Dickinson felt "defrauded" and that she harped repeatedly on the theme of loss, now as an ultimate, lifelong loss. Therefore, Dickinson seems to answer Gilbert and Gubar's claim that the poetry was enough with a counterclaim that indeed it was not.

Still, Gilbert and Gubar (1979) insist that it is the male literary and psychoanalytic critics, such as Richard Sewall (1974) and John Cody (1971), who are mistaken when they question how Dickinson's life might have been different if she had married. They condemn any skepticism about their own belief that poetry can be "enough" for lifelong self-fulfillment. They seem to be dazzled by the brilliance of the poetry and the mystique of creative inspiration and its intensity.

It is true that to live within the intensity of creative self-expression is a uniquely enhancing aspect of life, and to be deprived of such expression due to sociological conditions would be a great tragedy. Many women may be inhibited by societal norms that require an overly nurturant and maternal role to dominate over acts of self-expression, so that time for such self-expression is often minimized or excluded. Yet, even during the height of the patriarchal Victorian era, many women who wished to write did so, and they did not have to renounce men and relationships to do it. Women whose creativity thrived with heterosexual relationships during the Victorian age included: Elizabeth Barrett Browning, who married Robert Browning; George Eliot, who lived with the literary critic, George Henry Lewes; and the novelist and biographer Elizabeth Gaskell, who was married throughout her adulthood. Woodman (1982), a Jungian analyst, explicitly states that Elizabeth Barrett Browning's poetry improved when she left her father's house to marry Browning. This is particularly interesting in light of the fact that Emily Dickinson's poetry dried up after a brilliant creative period which Cody (1971) has connected with the acute and traumatic chaos of a psychotic break. With continued withdrawal from the world, the object relations necessary to fuel creative expression were lacking, and as her psychotic brilliance turned to schizoid control, her poetry suffered. Yet, late in her life, Dickinson had a revival of creative inspiration and productivity (Sewall, 1974), which coincided with her platonic love affair with her then deceased father's male friend, Judge Otis T. Lord. Her latent heterosexual desires apparently came free from their incestuous attachment to a paternal internal object, and Dickinson was impelled to write her most erotically suggestive poem.

Wild Nights—Wild Nights!
Were I with thee
Wild Nights should be
Our luxury!

Futile—the Winds—
To a Heart in port—
Done with the Compass—
Done with the Chart!

Rowing in Eden—
Ah, the Sea!
Might I but moor—Tonight—
In Thee!

Complete Poems, #249

Society may make it difficult for women to write, but to generalize patriarchal restrictions to the fear that relations with men are, in themselves, prohibitive for female creativity is a denial of the object relations issues involved. Dickinson was inspired toward creative work by her feelings for a man, and her refusal to marry him came from deep and early fears of dominance by a maternal object threatening to extinguish her sense of self.

By contrast, we have another female literary figure of the Victorian age, Charlotte Bronte, a novelist who wrote the classic works *Jane Eyre* and *Villette*. *Villette,* in particular, depicts a Victorian-age woman's successful efforts to overcome male opposition to her authentic self-expression. It is a vivid portrayal of a woman's fight to create her own identity. Bronte was certainly impinged on by her society. Although her father encouraged her and her siblings' literary expressions, he also, perhaps dutifully, kept reminding her that "woman's work" must come first. When she wrote for encouragement of her efforts at poetry to a then well-known literary personality, England's poet laureate, Robert Southey, she was pointedly rebuked (Gaskell, 1857; Peters, 1986). She was told that although her verses did indeed have merit, her inspirations must be confined to a corner of her life, a corner in the kitchen, where she might write while she waited for her dough to rise. Essentially, he reminded her of her "god-given" domestic role.

Yet, Charlotte Bronte published four novels, in addition to producing her early journals of poetry, prose, and drama, and her later poetic verses. In *Villette* she made us aware of the bleeding pain of unrequited love as perhaps we have never known it before, particularly from a woman's point of view. She also wrote about how a woman can transform and restore a man to his innate tender capacities for relationships. And she did not neglect to include how a man can simultaneously transform a woman, by inviting her assertive aggression to emerge. Bronte did not give up her feminine self, nor did she give up her creativity, although she had to hide behind a male pseudonym to publish. In the end, she didn't give up an opportunity to marry either. She was married for a year before she died of a complex of tuberculosis and pregnancy complications. Toward the end, she began to talk to her husband about her plans to write another novel. Her husband was controlling in many ways, yet he encouraged her to write.

The Odds Against Creative Women

Besides sociological thorns, there are also psychological thorns in the sides of women. Greenacre (1960) writes that there have been more distinguished male artists than women, and that those women who have become distinguished in the arts generally didn't have children. This observation is disillusioning, but again it implies sociological factors. Perhaps women with children just don't have the time to write?

A look at the psychological implications is more disturbing than settling for a sociological explanation of women's roles and responsibilities. Do women choose childcare to the exclusion of creative self-expression because they feel more adequate in nurturing another self than in defining their own unique self? Do women fear the psychic incest aspects of a creative rendezvous with their internal fathers, because, as in Dickinson's case and in the case of Ms. T, it might be so psychologically compelling?

Other major points made by Greenacre also prompt distressing questions. She believes that women fail to cultivate their creative capacities for two main reasons. First, she states that creativity requires the dominance of phallic character qualities that could seriously threaten a woman's feminine identity. Second, she states that little girls have to become too polite to have the grandiose confidence of the creative personality, since their oedipal stage, unlike that of boys, requires that they negotiate with the same parental figure with whom they are now competing, since a little girl continues to depend on her mother for care even as she feels intense rivalry toward her. Both these points put women at a severe disadvantage where creativity is concerned. However, are they valid?

The first point seems based on the fallacious reasoning that creativity is more phallic than feminine. The father's mirroring may play a great role in motivating a little girl toward creative efforts, but if he does give her positive mirroring, he is affirming her femininity as well as her movement toward creative self-expression. Even if Jungians, such as Monick (1929), are right, and a phallic force is at work in promoting creative efforts, the emergence of creative expression requires as much feminine gestative qualities as it requires phallic expounding qualities. Judy Chicago (1977) is an artist who has been a leader in defining how feminine creativity is unique and need not be imitative of masculine art.

Greenacre's second point is more disturbing. Are we, as women, truly the victims of oedipal level politics? This point may have some validity in that little girls change love objects, and therefore must negotiate relations with mother as they turn toward father. Still, is it valid to assume that being politic need crush creativity? On the contrary, it might promote it, as certainly seems true in the case of Emily Dickinson, where her outward compliance with her father, and in varying ways with both parents, prompted an intense need for her to express her aggression through her secret transitional world of poetic creation. External politics in relations might just as well lead to creative expression as to repression. Much would also depend on the particular mother and father involved, and the internalizations and identifications from relations with these two particular parents. Greenacre speaks from the stereotyped format of development prompted by drive theory and doesn't allow the latitude needed to capture the wide range of developmental phenomena produced by varying object relations dynamics. The view that a little girl would have to suppress her creativity is reminiscent of the same axioms Greenacre employs when she declares that phallic dominance is necessary for creative expression. Once she assumes this, it is simply the next step to say that self-exhibition at the phallic stage must be sustained rather than squelched at the oedipal stage in order for creative self-expression to be promoted. However, if we don't accept the first premise, we don't have to accept the second. Further, little boys who perpetuate phallic or grandiose exuberance might very well not be at all artistically creative, although they might fear outward interpersonal risks less than little girls who have to be politically constrained. Overall, it appears that Greenacre's view of what creativity is is too limiting. She doesn't appreciate how creativity can be enriched and even generated by bisexual desires, nor how suppressed phallic aggression might mobilize creativity, particularly in women.

Gedo (1983) devotes one of 12 chapters of his book to a discussion of female creativity, while all his other chapters portray male artists. In his chapter on females, he, like Greenacre, has cautious words for women. He speaks about maternal and paternal envy being directed more toward female children than toward males, and informs us that such parental envy inhibits creative development. He claims that mothers are, of course, envious of their daughters due to oedipal rivalry, but that fathers are also envious of their daughters more than of their sons, because their sons' accomplishments are seen as narcissistic reflections of their own greatness, while the gender differentiation of their daughters does not lend itself to such narcissistic reflection for fathers. One wonders why mothers might not be seen as desiring their daughters to accomplish in order to reflect their greatness. Of course, a more fundamental question is: Why does Gedo believe that narcissistic mirroring of the parents is the chief determinant of whether children fulfill their creative ambitions? Parents who affirm their children in all aspects of their self-expression, responding interactively and empathically to all their children's feelings, not just to their supposed "talents," might be more likely to promote artistic qualities as well as all other forms of creativity in their children (see Winnicott, 1971, on "creative living").

Although neither Greenacre nor Gedo are optimistic about the cultivation of creative talent in women, Greenacre does acknowledge one highly determinant factor that can tip the balance in favor of the creative woman. It is the same factor that can play such a dominant role in promoting creative addiction in women. It is the factor of the father's effect on his female child's creative strivings.

Greenacre concludes that female children who are lucky enough to have fathers who are artists are often encouraged by such fathers to develop their own talents. If these girls are not actually encouraged by the father, they can promote their own talents through identifications with their artistic fathers. Tessman's research (1989) with highly successful and creative women at MIT corroborates such a speculation. Tessman presents numerous case examples of the father's major influence on the mode of female intellectual development. She emphasizes the father's capacity during the oedipal stages of female development and beyond to have permeable boundaries so as to allow a daughter's experience of her father's thinking processes and internal self-activation. The father's interactive responsiveness to his daughter's creative endeavors, as well as his permeability and availability in sharing his own intellectual processes, are complementary components of the father's impact on a daughter's intellectual and creative development.

Tessman's findings corroborate my own clinical and psychobiographical research findings in that they allow my conclusion that the father is a chief motivational force in female creative development, regardless of the immense impact of mothering on the development of innate creative capacity. Like Tessman, I believe that the female ego-ideal is greatly affected by oedipal stage heterosexual desires, with desire prompting secure internalization of identifications, as well as internalization of positive mirroring objects.

Summary

This chapter attempts to formulate some of the major factors that affect female creative development. Intrapsychic fantasies have been cited as fundamental to both the emergence of female creative expression and its pathological vicissitudes, particularly in relation to creative addiction. The internal father and internally recorded relations with him have been seen as constituting one main intrapsychic constellation around which female creative expression psychically organizes. Emily Dickinson illustrates an extreme of addiction in relation to female creativity that can be seen in other women as well, such as in the case of Ms. T.

Sociological factors affecting the cultivation of creative expression in women are also considered. The ability of female creative motivation to surpass sociological obstacles is demonstrated in the example of Charlotte Bronte. Further considerations of creative development in women are addressed in response to the prior literature in this area, as most prominently represented by the two psychoanalysts Phyllis Greenacre and John Gedo.

References

Bronte, C. (1985). *Jane Eyre.* In S. M. Gilbert & S. Gubar (Eds.), *The Norton anthology of literature by women.* New York: W. W. Norton.

Bronte, C. (1985). *Villette.* New York: Penguin Books.

Chicago, J. (1977). *Through a flower.* New York: Bantam Books.

Cody, J. (1971). *After great pain.* Cambridge MA: Harvard University Press.

Dickinson, E. (1960). *The complete poems of Emily Dickinson* (T. H. Johnson, ed.). Boston: Little, Brown.

Gaskell, E. (1857). *The life of Charlotte Bronte.* New York: Penguin Books, 1983.

Gedo, J. (1983). *Portraits of the artist.* New York: Guilford Press.

Gerin, W. (1971). *Emily Bronte.* New York: Oxford University Press.

Gilbert, S. M., & Gubar, S. (1979). *Madwoman in the attic.* New Haven: Yale University Press.

Greenacre, P. (1960). Woman as artist. In *Emotional Growth I* (pp. 575–591). New York: International Universities Press.

Guntrip, H. (1976). *Schizoid phenomena, object relations and the self.* New York: International Universities Press.

Hatfield, C. W. (1941). *The complete poems of Emily Jane Bronte.* New York: Columbia University Press.

Kavaler, S. (1985). Mirror, mirror on the wall. . . *Journal of Comprehensive Psychotherapy, 4,* 1–38.

Kavaler, S. (1986). Lord of the mirrors and the demon lover. *American Journal of Psychoanalysis, 46*(4), 336–344.

Kavaler, S. (1988). Diane Arbus and the demon lover. *American Journal of Psychoanalysis, 48*(4) 366–370.

Kavaler, S. (1989). Ann Sexton and the daimonic lover. *American Journal of Psychoanalysis, 49*(1), 105–114.

Kavaler-Adler, S. (1991). Emily Dickinson and the subject of seclusion. *American Journal of Psychoanalysis, 51*(1), 21–38.

Kavaler-Adler, S. (in press). *The compulsion to create; a psychoanalytic study.*

Masterson, J. (1972). *Psychotherapy of the borderline adult: A developmental approach.* New York: Brunner/Mazel.

Masterson, J. (1981). *The narcissistic and borderline disorders.* New York: Brunner/Mazel

McNeil, H. (1986). *Emily Dickinson.* New York: Random House.

Modell, A. (1975). A narcissistic defense against affects and the illusion of self-sufficiency. *International Journal of Psychoanalysis, 56,* 275–282.

Modell, A. (1976). The holding environment and the therapeutic action of psychoanalysis. *Journal of the American Psychoanalytic Association, 24,* 285–308.

Monick, E. (1929). *Phallos, sacred image of the masculine.* Toronto: Inner City Books.

Peters, M. (1986). *A biography of Charlotte Bronte.* New York: Atheneum.

Plath, S. (1961). *Ariel.* New York: Harper & Row.

Rich, A. (1979). *On lies, secrets, and silence.* New York: W. W. Norton.

Sewall, R. B. (1980). *The life of Emily Dickinson.* New York: Farrar, Straus & Giroux.

Tessman, L. H. (1989). Fathers and daughters: Early tones, later echoes. In S. H. Cath, A. Gurwitt, & L. Gunsberg (Eds.), *Fathers and their families* (pp. 197–224). Hillsdale, NJ: Analytic Press.

Ward, T. V. W. (1961). *The capsule of the mind: Chapters in the life of Emily Dickinson.* Cambridge, MA: Harvard University Press.

Winnicott, D. W. (1965). *The maturational processes and the facilitating environment.* New York: International Universities Press.

Winnicott, D. W. (1971). *Playing and reality.* Middlesex, England: Penguin Books.

Wolff, C. G. (1985). *Emily Dickinson.* New York: Alfred A. Knopf.

Woodman, M. (1962). *Addiction to perfection, the still unravished bride.* Toronto: Inner City Books.

Woolf, V. (1929). *A room of one's own.* London: Hogarth Press.

Thumbelina and the Development of Female Sexuality

Sidney M. Rosenblatt, Ph.D.

This chapter will explore the meaning and importance of fairy tales in the development of female sexual identity using Hans Christian Andersen's tale "Thumbelina" as an illustration. In his seminal work, *The Uses of Enchantment: The Meaning and Importance of Fairy Tales,* Bruno Bettelheim (1976) provides a manifesto for the psychoanalytic study of fairy tales:

> Because the child's life is often bewildering to him, the child needs even more to be given the chance to understand himself in the complex world in which he must learn to cope. To be able to do so, the child must be helped to make some coherent sense out of the turmoil of his feelings. He needs ideas on how to bring his inner house into order, and on that basis be able to create order in his life. The child finds this kind of meaning through fairy tales. (p. 5)

Like many other modern psychological insights, this one was anticipated long ago by poets, and Bettelheim quotes the 18th century author Schiller, who says, "Deeper meaning resides in fairy tales told to me in my childhood than in the truth that is taught by life." Bettelheim continues:

> Through the centuries if not millennia, during which in their retelling fairy tales become ever-more refined, they come to convey at the same time overt and covert meanings, come to speak simultaneously to all levels of the human personality, communicating in a manner which reaches the uneducated mind of

> the child as well as that of the sophisticated adult. Applying the psychoanalytic model of the human personality, fairy tales carry important messages to the conscious, the pre-conscious, and the unconscious mind on whatever level each is functioning at the time. By dealing with universal human problems, particularly those which preoccupy the child's mind, these stories speak to his budding ego, and encourage its development, while at the same time reliving pre-conscious and unconscious pressures. As the stories unfold, they give conscious credence and body to id pressures, and show ways to satisfy these that are in line with ego and superego requirements. (p. 5)

Bettelheim's interest in fairy tales grew out of his desire to understand why so many children—normal and abnormal, intelligent and dull—find folk tales and fairy tales more satisfying than all other children's literature. As he studied fairy tales' great success in enriching children's inner lives, he came to realize that these stories start where children really are in their psychological and emotional beings. Fairy tales speak about children's "severe inner pressures in a way that the child unconsciously understands, and, without belittling the most serious inner struggles which growing up entails, offer examples of both temporary and permanent solutions to pressing difficulties." Bettelheim contends that "a proper understanding of the unique merit of fairy tales will induce parents and teachers to assign them once again to that central role in the life of the child they held for centuries."

"Thumbelina" is illustrative as a vehicle for helping the young girl resolve the developmental difficulties of her journey towards womanhood. I became aware of Andersen's tale through my daughter, who greatly enjoys having it read to her, as well as reading it herself.

> Once upon a time, there was a woman who longed for a little child of her own, but she had no idea where she could get one. So off she went to see an old witch, and she said to her, "I'd so much like to have a little child. Won't you please tell me where I can get one?"
>
> "Why, yes. That is no trouble at all," said the witch. "You must take this grain of barley. It's not the kind that grows in the farmer's field or that hens eat, either. Put it in a flower pot, and then wait and see what happens."
>
> "Oh, thank you, kindly," said the woman. She gave the witch a shilling, and then went home and planted the grain of barley.
>
> A beautiful, big flower sprang up at once. It looked very much like a tulip, but the petals were tightly closed as though it were still in bud. "What a pretty flower it is," said the woman, kissing its beautiful red and yellow petals. But just as she kissed

> it, the flower suddenly burst open. You could see it was a real tulip now, but right in the middle of the flower, on a green stool, sat a tiny, little girl, delicate and lovely. She was not above an inch tall, and so, she was called Thumbelina.
>
> She was given a splendid, lacquered walnut shell as her cradle. Blue violet petals formed her mattress and a rose petal her eiderdown. There she slept at night. But during the day, she played on the table, where the woman had set a plate with a wreath of flowers arranged around the edge so the stalks lay in the water. On the surface, a large tulip petal floated, and Thumbelina could sit in it and sail from one side of the plate to the other. She had two white horsehairs to row with. It looked very pretty indeed. She could sing, too, so daintily and charmingly, that no one ever heard the like.

Thumbelina may be analyzed as a story of female masturbation. The "tiny, little girl, delicate and lovely" represents the clitoris, and through masturbation the child discovers her body and her femininity. In a masturbatory reverie, floating on a petal and singing, she begins to discover her body ego boundaries and her sense of self—through playing with her hand, using her thumb to play with the "tiny, little girl."

> However, one night as she lay in her beautiful bed, an ugly, old toad came hopping in through the window where there was a broken pane of glass. The toad looked very big and wet and ugly, as she hopped straight down onto the petal where Thumbelina lay asleep under her red rose petal.

Thumbelina clearly represents the clitoris, and the red rose petals the lips of the vagina.

> "She'd make a nice wife for my son," said the toad. And so, she took hold of the walnut shell where Thumbelina was sleeping, and hopped off with her through the broken pane down into the garden. Down at the bottom flowed a big, broad stream, and close by the bank the ground was marshy and muddy. Here the toad lived with her son. Ugh! He was ugly and repulsive, too, and looked exactly like his mother. "Croak, croak, croak," was all he could say when he saw the charming little girl in the walnut shell.
>
> "Don't talk so loud, or she'll wake," said the old toad. "She could still run away from us, for she's as light as swansdown. We'll put her out on the stream on one of the broad waterlily leaves. She's so light and small, it'll seem like an island to her. She won't be able to run away from there. And in the meantime, we'll

> spring clean the best room down under the mud, and you shall settle down and live there together."

The masturbatory fantasy leads to feelings of disgust and fear at the need to deal with the gross physical world of intercourse, pregnancy, and childbirth, which are seen by the young child as being forced to marry a toad. The girl must give up infantile masturbation—floating amidst flower petals—for becoming involved in adult physical sexuality, conceptualized as wallowing in mud.

> The poor little thing woke quite early in the morning. And when she saw where she was, she began to cry bitterly. For there was water all around the big, green leaf, and she had no way at all of getting to land. The old toad sat down below the mud, decorating her room with rushes and yellow waterflowers to make it neat and pretty for her new daughter-in-law. Then she swam out with her ugly son to the leaf where Thumbelina was standing. They had come to fetch her pretty bed, which they wanted to have ready in the bride's bedroom before she came. The old toad bowed deeply in the water to her, and said, "This is my son you see with me. He's going to be your husband, and the two of you shall have a very nice place to live in down below in the mud." But all the son could say was "Croak, croak, croak."

Thumbelina then escapes from the old toad and her son, being carried away by a little, white butterfly—symbolic of the child's budding genitals. In other words, with growing womanhood, the toad can be conquered. Thumbelina has a series of adventures, first living with birds in the forest, then with a field mouse, and next with a mole who wishes to marry her. However, she cannot bear to be married to a mole. She befriends a swallow, whose life she saves, and the swallow carries her away.

> "The cold winter is coming on now," said the swallow, "and I'm flying far away to a warmer land. Will you come with me? You can sit on my back and bind yourself fast with your sash. Then we shall fly away from the nasty mole and his dark home, far away, over the mountains, to warm lands, where the sun shines more beautifully than it does here, where there is always summer and lovely flowers. Do fly away with me, dear little Thumbelina. You saved my life when I lay frozen in the dark cellar under the earth."
>
> "Yes, I'll go with you," said Thumbelina. And she seated herself upon the bird's back with her feet resting on its outstretched wings, and tied her belt firmly to one of its strongest feathers.

And so the swallow flew high up into the air, over forest and lake, high up over the great mountains where the snow always lies. Thumbelina froze in the cold air, but she crept under the bird's warm feathers, and only popped her head out to see all the beautiful scenery below her. So they came to the warm lands where the sun shines much more brightly than it does here. The sky seemed twice as high, and along the ditches and hedges grew the loveliest green and blue grapes. Oranges and lemons hung in the woods scented with myrtle and mint. And along the country lanes, lovely children ran and played with great, brightly colored butterflies. But the swallow flew further still, and everything grew more and more beautiful. Under magnificent green trees by a blue lake stood a palace built in ancient times of shining white marble with vines entwined around its tall pillars. Right on top of the pillars were many swallows' nests. And in one of them lived the swallow that carried Thumbelina.

"Here's my house," said the swallow. "But if you will choose yourself one of those lovely flowers growing down there, I will set you down on it. And you will live as happily there as you could wish."

"That would be lovely," she said, clapping her little hands.

A great white marble column lay fallen on the ground. It was broken into three pieces, and between them grew the most beautiful white flowers. The swallow flew down with Thumbelina, and set her upon one of the broad petals. But what a surprise she had. There, in the middle of the flower, sat a little man, clear and transparent like glass. He had the prettiest golden crown upon his head, and the loveliest bright wings upon his shoulders. And he himself was no bigger than Thumbelina. He was the guardian spirit of the flower. In every flower there lived a little man or woman just like him, but he was king over them all.

"Oh, how beautiful he is," whispered Thumbelina to the swallow.

The little prince was quite frightened of the swallow, for it was such an enormous bird by the side of this dainty, little creature. But when he saw Thumbelina, he was overjoyed, for she was quite the most beautiful girl he had ever seen. And so, he took the golden crown off his own head, and placed it upon hers. He asked her what she was called, and said that if she would be his wife, she should be queen over all the flowers. Well, that was a husband indeed. Quite a different matter from the toad's son and the mole with the black velvet fur. And so she said yes to the handsome prince. From every flower appeared a little lady or gentleman so beautiful and dainty it was a joy to look at them. And everyone brought Thumbelina a present, but the best of all was the pair of beautiful wings from a large white fly. They were fastened upon Thumbelina's shoulders, and then she too could fly from flower to flower. They were all so full of joy.

And the swallow sat up above in its nest and sang for them as well as it could. But it was very sad at heart, for it was so fond of Thumbelina that it wanted never to be parted from her.

"You cannot be called Thumbelina," the flower sprite said to her. "It's an ugly name, and you are so beautiful. We shall call you Maia."

"Goodbye, goodbye," said the swallow, and flew away from the warm lands once more, far away, back to Denmark.

"Thumbelina" is the story of the child's masturbatory life. The child first masturbates, discovering her clitoris—represented by the tiny lovely girl born without any difficulties of pregnancy or childbirth. Through her discovery and new knowledge, the child develops a body-ego that allows her to confront the fears of adult physicality that are awakened by the very fact of masturbation and her learning about the body. Through masturbation, the child comes to know the difference between the anal and the vaginal openings, between the mole and the prince, and this is an essential step in the child's sexual development.

Marie Bonaparte (1953) states that the difference between vagina and anus is unclear to the infant girl, and that the child's ability to conceptualize her feminine identity as deriving from clitoral stimulation, vaginal intercourse, pregnancy, and giving birth, rather than through anal excretory processes, is an important developmental phase. She writes:

> Women are often afraid of motherhood, and not only for economic reasons, which may also incite men to avoid procreation, for they dread the pain and danger that offsets the otherwise deep-rooted instinct to bear children. . . . I cannot too much insist, however, that in childhood even girls do not truly vaginally apprehend the orifice which the penis is to penetrate, that is, with a clear representation of the recto-vaginal septum. Doubtless this orifice is then cloacally conceived, even if already discovered by the small fingers. True, the girl possesses an anatomical foundation for the concept of the vagina hole, which the boy lacks. But unlike ordinary holes—passages which already serve some purpose, such as the mouth, ears, nostrils, and anus—the vagina, through which nothing has so far passed, cannot doubtless be ideated so early as having an own and separate role. The horror, above all, of being castrated, of which the vulva would be the mark of the wound, must help to ward off from the girl any precise observation of this region." (pp. 49–50)

Through the fairy tale of Thumbelina, the girl, on a deep unconscious level, begins to make the separation between the anal and the vaginal opening, so that she can visualize herself as having the power to conceive and does not have to spend her life with the mole in the anal region of her body. Instead, she is made ruler, given wings to fly, and changes her name.

Marie Bonaparte also states that, as part of infantile sexuality, the female child experiences birth and pregnancy as alimentary functions, and that birth occurs through the anus rather than through the vagina. It is my feeling that the fairy tale of Thumbelina helps the little girl see herself as being able to have children through the vagina rather than through the anus.

Bruno Bettelheim's work on fairy tales, and my interest in "Thumbelina," focus primarily on sexual development as described by the early, classical psychoanalytic writers. However, more modern psychoanalytic writers on female sexuality take issue with the classical view. Elaine Siegel (1988) reports that modern writers, including Kleeman, Gailison, Roiphe, and Stoller, describe the existence of vaginal awareness between 14 and 24 months; this contributes to gender identity formation and a sense of femaleness at a preoedipal age. Siegel also notes that as early as 1932, Brierley presented clinical evidence that females have sensations in the vagina at an early age. In 1935, Greenacre and Kernberg's research substantiated early vaginal sensations, and postulated an inner genital phase at approximately two to four years of age. Siegel quotes from Kestenberg's 1982 work:

> The early inner genital phase begins with a disequilibrium in which pre-genital drives and early genital drives and derivative ego functions vie with one another. The ensuing integration of pre-genital and phallic drives and applied ego functions, under the aegis of inner genitality, is aided by the child's identification with the mother, who acts as an external organizer, reinforcing and guiding inner genitality, the inner or internal organizer at the time. Externalization of inner genital impulses is the mechanism which underlies their sublimation into maternal behavior and the wish to be a mother. The former dyadic relationship is now replaced by a triangular girl-baby-mother relationship. (p. 3)

Siegel goes on to say:

> Kestenberg believes that the inner genital phase deeply influences each developmental phase, and is the basis for later maternal behavior and for the vaginal slow-spreading type of sensual excitation, but since, in essence, the inner genital phase is one of disequilibrium, the developmental task has to be the integration of tensions, excitations, and urges and impulses then

> vaguely perceived. But Kestenberg feels that inner genital sensations yield no product; therefore, they need to be externalized and made into a living link with mother. Kestenberg sees such integration as taking place in the externalization of kinesthetic and visual memories in playing. Doll play is seen by her as the principal outlet. (p. 3)

Further, Siegel reports that in her homosexual patients, there was a conspicuous absence of doll play in the patients' early developmental histories.

The question is: How do we reconcile the ideas of Bonaparte and the ideas of the classical psychoanalytic model of female sexuality with the newer model of female sexuality as presented by Siegel? I think one way of resolving the problem is to admit that both developmental stages occur equally. The female child does need to distinguish between anal and vaginal sensations, even though she is aware of vaginal sensations as early as 14 months, because she is also at the same time aware of anal sensations, and she may very easily confuse these two types of sensations, especially at an early age.

To form an adequate sense of the bodily self, the girl must distinguish between anal and vaginal sensations, and must conceptualize the vaginal sensations as the source of female sexual identity. The distinction between vagina and anus also contributes to the formation of ego identity, since the ego is essentially a body-ego. Therefore, even though the preoedipal child is aware of many vaginal sensations, the knowledge gained through Thumbelina allows the child an opportunity to conquer developmental fears through working out the distinction between vaginal and anal stimulation.

The case history of Karen elucidates the clinical use of the "Thumbelina" fairy tale, with the client moving from an anal to a genital orientation. Karen, a 27-year-old tax accountant, entered analysis because of depression. Despite many years of dating, she was unable to form an emotionally connected relationship with a mate. She did, however, feel emotionally committed to her many girlfriends. She and her friends were continually in deep psychological crises of one sort or another, and they offered each other a great deal of help and support.

Karen had one older brother, and she was very close to her mother. Her father, a teacher, had died of a heart attack when Karen was four years old. Both the client and her mother had suffered from constipation for many years and relied on suppositories to provide relief. At the time of entering therapy, Karen and her mother were still quite concerned with their digestive functioning and bowel movements. As Karen grew up, an involved ritual had developed around taking suppositories for alleviating constipation, with both mother and daughter informing each other about taking medication, then waiting until the suppository melted inside the body, and finally having their bowel movement. Karen likened the whole procedure to a ritual dance.

Soon after beginning therapy, the client had a series of vivid dreams in which she made love to one of her girlfriends. Soon thereafter, Karen began having a sexual relationship with this friend in actuality. The "affair" did not last long, being more of an experiment than a genuine emotional or physical commitment. Nevertheless, the relationship with the girlfriend afforded the client pleasure, and seemed to be a way of acting out her intense attachment to the mother.

Karen then became involved with a man who behaved quite abusively toward her but who was sexually satisfying and exciting for her. In this relationship, which lasted about two years, the client talked about and acted out a number of masochistic fantasies. After ending this involvement, Karen began a long-term relationship with a nonabusive, professional man. The client subsequently married this man, and they later had a baby.

This case history vignette exemplifies the movement from anal-genital orientation to purely genital involvement. The primary relationship with the mother is an anal involvement. The involvement then becomes genital through a series of stages: first, lovemaking with a female; then, lovemaking with an abusive male (who also unconsciously represents the mother); and finally, lovemaking with a caring and supportive male. In "Thumbelina," we also find the suggestion that the early anal involvement is with the mother, and that the migration from anal to genital stimulation occurs in a step-wise fashion, moving from representations of the mother to representations of the father. It is suggested that the girl's psychosexual development, in which the relationship with the mother is transformed to an involvement with the father, parallels and is related to the maturation from an anal-genital to a more exclusively genital orientation.

References

Andersen, H. C. (1985). *Hans Andersen's fairy tales* (Ed. & trans. L. W. Kingsland). London: Oxford University Press.

Bettelheim, B. (1976). *The uses of enchantment: The meaning and importance of fairy tales.* New York: Knopf.

Bonaparte, M. (1953). *Female sexuality.* London: Imago.

Siegel, E. V. (1988). *Female homosexuality: Choice without volition: A psychoanalytic study.* Hillsdale, NJ: The Analytic Press.

The Forbidden Room: A Pair of Fairy Tales as Developmental Metaphor

Penny W. Caccavo, M.S.W.

The forbidden room, a theme that resonates with suspense and sometimes horror in many a fairy tale, still fascinates adults as well as children. While the tale that comes to mind is usually "Bluebeard," and while there are related tales—"Mr. Fox" (Steel, 1918), "Fitcher's Bird" (Grimm, 1944)—in which the room is forbidden to a young woman by her surly husband or fiancé, there are other tales in which it is not a man but a maternal figure who forbids the heroine to enter the secret room. And while the most lastingly popular fairy tales feature a good (but dead) mother and an evil stepmother, or a good fairy and a witch, in the tales I am about to describe, the mother figure is both benign and adversarial. Furthermore, even though the surface theme may appear oedipal—an older and a younger woman struggle, and in the end the younger one marries a king—the real struggle here is the preoedipal one of a girl's efforts to achieve independence from her mother's domination. Every young girl must pass through this stage, in which the exhilaration of autonomy becomes stronger than fear of mother's disapproval, as a prerequisite to competition for a man. At the crisis there is an uncanny feeling about these tales, a sense that the girl may lose her struggle and be drawn forever backward into thralldom. Her right to full womanhood is quite literally at stake.

"Mother Hildegarde," from Howard Pyle's 19th century collection, *The Wonder Clock,* begins with the remarriage of a king, after his wife's death, to a woman who would like to replace his daughter with her own. The stepmother pushes the princess into a well, from the bottom of which she emerges into the realm of Mother Hildegarde, whose bellows make the winds blow on Earth and whose laundry sprinkling causes the rain. The princess promises to serve her faithfully in return for food and lodging, and all goes well until Mother Hildegarde goes off on a journey, giving the princess her keys and the freedom of the house *except for one room,* which she must not enter or "I will be sure to know it, and ill-luck will be certain to happen to you" (Pyle, 1887, p. 194).

Of course, curiosity overcomes her. First she just looks at the door, next she inserts the key in the lock, and finally she opens the door to find a room containing only a tall covered jar. Peeping into it she sees only water. But at the bottom, far away, she sees Mother Hildegarde looking at her. Too late she slaps the jar shut and flees the room. A strand of her hair has touched the water, and all her hair turns to pure gold. Mother Hildegarde returns and questions her three times, but the princess denies everything, in spite of her telltale hair. So her protectress strikes her dumb and isolates her in a great forest, where she lives in the trees and eventually has nothing to wear but her long golden hair, which she weaves about her.

The months go by and eventually a young king finds her while hunting, takes her home even though she cannot speak, and marries her over his mother's objections. But Mother Hildegarde appears to the young queen after the birth of her first child, restores her speech, and asks her again whether she entered the forbidden room. Again the princess denies, so Mother Hildegarde takes away not only her speech but her baby as well and smears her lips with blood. This happens three times, after which the king is prevailed upon to have her burned at the stake as a witch. As the flames mount, Mother Hildegarde appears with the three children and questions her once more. The princess finally confesses, whereupon rain falls, putting out the fire, and all is forgiven.

The second tale is "Our Lady's Child" from *The Complete Grimm's Fairy Tales,* collected in the early 19th century from carriers of old oral traditions. The Virgin Mary takes the little daughter of a poor couple and raises her in heaven. When the girl is 14, Mary goes on a journey, leaving her the keys of "the thirteen doors of heaven" and telling her she may open all but the thirteenth, which "is forbidden you." Her curiosity grows until she can no longer resist the temptation to put the key in the lock, whereupon the door springs open, revealing "the Trinity sitting in fire and splendor . . . then she touched the light a little with her finger, and her finger became quite golden (Grimm, 1944, pp.

24–25). Mary returns, questions the girl, who denies all in spite of her golden finger, and, after three times, Mary banishes her from heaven, and she finds herself speechless in a thorny wilderness. She takes refuge in a hollow tree and is eventually without clothing except for her long naturally golden hair.

Years pass and a king discovers her, takes her home even though she cannot talk, and marries her. When her first child is born, Mary appears, asks her to confess, and takes away both speech and baby when she denies. After the third disappearance, the people assume the young queen has devoured her children, and she is condemned to be burned. When the fire has started, she wishes she could confess; her voice returns, she confesses, rain falls, and Mary appears with the three children and forgives her wholeheartedly.

Freud, Jung, and Rank have all attested to the timelessness, cross-cultural similarity and symbolic significance of myths and fairy tales. Melanie Klein (1921), Ella Freeman Sharpe (1937) and Bruno Bettelheim (1977) have attributed the continued popularity of fairy tales to their speaking to the unconscious. Bettelheim describes the girl child's use of splitting of the maternal object in her oedipal fantasy but emphasizes her "belief and trust in the goodness of the preoedipal mother" as mitigating the girl's rivalrous hostility and guilt toward the oedipal "(step)mother who stands in her way" (1977, p. 114). He does not take up the frightening preoedipal mother. In the two tales just recounted, defensive splitting is not successful, and the semibenign power of the chief mother figure is somewhat fearsome. But neither is the heroine an all-good, totally passive little cipher as in so many fairy tales. I would like to examine these tales as if they were dreams. Freud said in *Totem and Taboo,* "It seems quite possible to apply the psychoanalytic views derived from dreams to products of ethnic imagination such as myths and fairy tales" (1913a, p. 185). A dreamer may give personal associations to each element in a dream and follow their lead into the unconscious. With a folk or fairy tale, the researcher may associate to its elements via symbols found to be universal in psychoanalysis and Western culture. One may also associate parallels in other tales, myths, art, religion, and relevant psychoanalytic findings.

First, the princess in "Mother Hildegarde" is pushed into a well and seemingly drowned. This death can be seen as a wish to be reunited with her dead mother, a return to the womb, and the comfort and bliss in the arms of the mother of infancy and early childhood, which is followed by rebirth into a beautiful landscape—paradise in "Our Lady's Child"—both symbols for the mother's body, according to Freud (1916–1917, p. 160) and Abraham (1911, p. 29). Soon she becomes a happy helper to a reincarnated, powerfully idealized mother. There is a latency-period quiescence about this part of the story; in "Our Lady's Child," a more infantile, indulged quality: "There the child fared well, ate sugar-cakes, and drank sweet milk" (Grimm, 1944, p. 24).

Times passes, and mother leaves the girl in charge and issues her warning about the forbidden room and its key. Her curiosity begins to build. Freud (1905b) revealed the universality of the infant's pleasure in its own body and its evolving curiosity about the bodies of its parents and siblings. Melanie Klein wrote of the child's wish to explore the mother's body, "the 'land flowing with milk and honey,'" as arising "out of the child's aggressive sexual desires, greed, curiosity and love" and connected this to a later "desire to rediscover the mother of the early days" (1937, pp. 333–334). Hartmann, Piaget, and others assigned curiosity and exploration, at least in part, to conflict-free functions of the developing ego. In these tales, however, the urge is anything but conflict-free: the girl freely explores Mother Hildegarde's great, fine house, or the twelve "dwellings of the kingdom of heaven" (Grimm, 1944, p. 24), which may symbolize growth to age 12, the threshold of puberty, although she is described as 14 when she gets to the thirteenth door. "The reality of the young girl," write Robert Lane and Saralea Chazan, "retains the texture of a tapestry, where fibers are interwoven and quality is discerned by touching as well as looking" (1988, p. 10). The words in both fairy tales describe with real feeling the adolescent urge to masturbate: "She never wanted anything in all of her life as much as she wanted just to peep into that little room" (Pyle, 1887, p. 194); and "the desire in her heart was not stilled, but gnawed there and tormented her, and let her have no rest" (Grimm, 1944, p. 24). It is clear that it is no longer the mother's body that she craves to explore, as she might have wished to as a little girl, but her own—and her mother has given her a classic double message about that: Here is the key, but do not use it.

Now the heroine ceases to be the all-good, passive little mother's helper. She asserts herself, albeit secretly; she explores; she inserts the key in the lock and opens the door. While Freud (1916–1917) and others have consistently interpreted a key as a phallic symbol, in these tales it is clearly a symbol for the girl's own finger, which she inserts in her vulva, touches to her clitoris, opens her unexplored vagina. In thus moving toward possession of her genitals, she moves toward integration of a formerly secret part of herself into her body image (Siegel, 1988) in preparation for the future possibility of sexual intercourse and motherhood.

And what does she see? In the Pyle tale, a tall covered jar of water—a straightforward womb or vagina symbol—into which she peeps and sees Mother Hildegarde looking up at her from its depths as if to say, "This is my territory, not yours." In the Grimm's tale, she sees "the Trinity sitting in fire and splendor." What can this mean? While "Our Lady's Child" is presented as a Christian allegory about the Virgin Mary, its similarity to the Grimm's tale about Mother Hildegarde, who controls the wind and the rain, suggests an earlier origin and a female trinity. In his beautiful essay, "The Theme of the Three Caskets," Freud (1913c) associated the number three with the three chronological aspects of womanhood (birth, love, and death) as represented by the Three Fates, and explores similar trinities back to classical antiquity and beyond, to goddesses representing the Three Seasons (earlier than our present four). Edith Hamilton's *Mythology* (1942, p. 46) refers to the tri-form Earth Mother goddesses of ancient days: Selene of the sky, Artemis of the earth, Hecate of the underworld. E. O. James (1960, p. 86) discusses the triad Artemis (virgin), Aphrodite (lover), and Hera (mother). Robert Graves finds the triad Artemis, Aphrodite, and Hecate in ancient Greece (1960) and the Brigit triad in medieval Ireland: the Brigit of poetry, the Brigit of healing, and the Brigit of smithcraft (1966, p. 394). Edmund Leach (1988) adds to these the female trinity of modern Hinduism: Parvati (lover), Durga (protector), and Kali (death). He also cites the second to fourth century Christian Gnostic Gospels, which refer to the three Marys: the Virgin, her sister, and Mary Magdalene—finding in this triad a historical relationship to the earlier classical Mediterranean ones.

A further connection between the Virgin Mary and early goddesses is presented by Freud (1911b). At Ephesus in Asia Minor, an ancient cult of the Mother Goddess was replaced by the conquering Ionians in the eighth century B.C.E. with their own cult of Artemis (Diana). Eventually Jesus' apostle John was reputed to have brought the Virgin Mary to Ephesus, where her apparent identification by the Greeks with Artemis helped Christianity to become accepted. The first basilica to Mary was erected in the fourth century A.D., at Ephesus.* Mary's identification with ancient goddesses was also suggested by Jung (von Franz, 1964, p. 225), who wrote that "the Virgin Mary can be said to be a representation of the Great Mother archetype" (see also James, 1960, p. 106).

So, whereas in one tale the heroine sees Mother Hildegarde's face,

* According to Leach (1988), it may have been Mary Magdalene who was brought to Ephesus by John.

in the other a possibly female trinity. I would like to speculate that this signifies the girl's discovery that the core of her femaleness identifies her with awesome and ancient female power, power as yet forbidden her. She then goes further and *touches:* A hair "accidentally" touches the water and her entire head of hair turns gold, or she touches "the light a little with her finger" (Grimm, 1944, p. 26), which turns gold, and she becomes very frightened. There seems little doubt that the gold and the light signify brightness and heat, hence excitement, even orgasm—which is not understood and therefore feared. Peter Blos refers to "that libidinal diffusion that effects in the female the erotization of the body, especially its surface" (1967, p. 174) after puberty. The skin flushes; hence, the golden glow may represent *red,* the red of blushing in shame or in heat, the red of the redhead, the scarlet woman, the red of menstrual blood, which was once considered both taboo and of great value (Bettelheim, 1962, pp. 24–29, 136–138; Freud, 1913a, 1918). Also suggested here is the common fantasy among ill-informed girls that they have injured themselves by masturbating and thus caused their first menstrual bleeding (Freud, 1931, p. 233) as well as the fantasy that people can tell by looking at them that they are menstruating (and hence that they have been masturbating). The first-menstruation hypothesis seems confirmed by the age of the girl in "Our Lady's Child" (14) and by the fact that the forbidden room was the *thirteenth* room (unlucky or cursed number); this correlates with Bettelheim's pointing out that it was the thirteenth fairy who put "the curse" (an old term for menstruation) on the Sleeping Beauty—the thirteenth being the last 28-day or lunar month in the old thirteen-lunar-months year; the curse being that at age 15 she shall prick her finger, bleed, and die (1977, p. 232). The Sleeping Beauty, too, opened a secret door into a little room in which an old woman allowed her to prick her finger. It is worth noting here that in some ancient tribes, defloration of virgin girls was carried out by old women (Freud, 1918, p. 195). Perhaps at one time these old women were representatives of the Goddess; perhaps self-defloration (as could happen during masturbation) was forbidden.

By now we have a welter of possible meanings: those originating in ancient religious and folk customs, those of the reality of maternal prohibition, and those of the girl's conscious or unconscious fantasies about what is happening to her body and about her own wishes and fears in regard to her mother. Fantasy material may originate along three tributary pathways: the oedipal, the negative oedipal, and the preoedipal.

Adolescence is a time of forceful resurgence of unconscious incestuous yearnings of early childhood—for the girl, the wish to compete with and replace mother as "the fairest of them all." But there seems little suggestion of competition or comparison in the two tales under consideration. There is some hint of the negative oedipal wish for exclusive possession of the mother by the girl, projected onto the mother-figure (Freud, 1915, 1920, 1931). But the mother does not lock the girl away and keep her for herself as in Rapunzel—a plainly negative-oedipal tale, in which the competition is not between a younger and an older woman for a man, but between a man and an older woman for possession of the younger woman. It was Helene Deutsch (1932) who first pointed out that female homosexual love-making reproduces the mother-baby relationship. The poet Anne Sexton interpreted this theme in her poem "Rapunzel"*:

> As she grew older Mother Gothel thought:
> None but I will ever see her or touch her.
> She locked her in a tower without a door
> or a staircase. It had only a high window.
> When the witch wanted to enter she cried:
> Rapunzel, Rapunzel, let down your hair.
> Rapunzel's hair fell to the ground like a rainbow.
> It was as yellow as a dandelion
> and as strong as a dog leash.
> Hand over hand she shinnied up
> the hair like a sailor
> and there in the stone-cold room,
> as cold as a museum,
> Mother Gothel cried:
> Hold me, my young dear, hold me,
> and thus they played mother-me-do. (p. 40)

The negative oedipal wish can be seen as solely the daughter's fantasy or as promoted by the reality of the mother's behavior. Sanford Weimer applied the theme of the jealously possessive mother in Rapunzel to his treatment of a young woman enmeshed with her mother, seen as "an all-powerful, all-seeing, all-knowing, intrusive figure" (1978, p. 30).

Rapunzel too had golden hair—unusually long hair. In her "Tales of the Discovery of the Secret Treasure," Selma Fraiberg (1954) suggested the acquisition of gold as a symbol for incest; in Rapunzel it would be mother-daughter incest. Mother Gothel's jealousy is obvious

---

* "Rapunzel" from *Transformations* by Anne Sexton. Copyright © 1971 by Anne Sexton. Reprinted by permission of Houghton Mifflin Co.

when she cuts off Rapunzel's hair (removes her source of attraction to men, her power—castrates her in the manner of Delilah to Samson) and banishes her *after* the prince's intrusion. Mother Hildegarde and Our Lady, on the other hand, banish their maidens before any incursion by men, only because they disobediently indulged their curiosity about their own bodies and arrived at menarche. The girls are banished but not hoarded by the mothers for themselves; it is the daughter's independence that is frowned upon—a theme from the preoedipal separation-individuation phase of early childhood (Mahler, 1968).

Becoming an individual separate from the mother seemed, according to Mahler, Pine, and Bergman, to be "generally more difficult for girls than for boys, because the girls, upon the discovery of the sexual difference, tended to turn back to the mother, to blame her, to demand from her, to be disappointed in her, and still to be ambivalently tied to her" (1975, p. 106). One of the ways in which differentiation between self and maternal object may be facilitated, says Isidor Bernstein, is "by the perception of the stimulation as coming from the child's own body. The ability to reproduce the sensations autonomously . . . helps the child to perceive himself as a separate entity. Therefore, it may also be used defensively as a way of countering fears of incorporation or annihilation of self" characteristic of this period (1975, p. 57). Ludwig Eidelberg found that masturbation and its accompanying fantasies produce "a conscious feeling of being independent of an external object" (1945, p. 137).

Unfortunately, both reality and fantasy may interfere. Mothers and other caretakers often suppress masturbation, and the girl herself may inhibit the urge in disappointment over her own anatomy. Summarizing recent research on mother-infant interaction, Doris K. Silverman writes that "the infant female has more awareness of her mother's inner need states than does the male. . . . The female's increased sensitivity . . . may make her more vulnerable and fearful of her mother's negative states" (1987, pp. 210–211). Elaine V. Siegel finds, "When infantile vaginal sensations are not greeted by unconscious and conscious approval by the parents, the little girl must conclude that these sensations are not appropriate or may be harmful. Therefore, she is prohibited from using them to complete her body image" (1988, p. 23).

In addition to the inhibition of masturbation, there are other contributions from the environment to the thwarting of autonomy. Frances G. Wickes, a Jungian, wrote, "Unless the parent is able, from the beginning, to see the child as a separate entity there is danger that love will become a clutching force using the child to satisfy personal need or ambition" (1927, p. 90). The Jungians saw the child's fantasy of the "terrible mother" who would "swallow up his awakening individuality" as "the regressive pull of the unconscious" of the child to remain dependent and irresponsible in "the Garden of Eden" (Wickes, 1927, pp. 9–10). Hence, both the mother and the child itself can impede maturation. Mahler too described "the well-known parasitic, infantilizing mother who . . . needs to continue her overprotection beyond the stage where it is no longer beneficial. This attitude becomes a threat of engulfment" (1968, p. 146).

Issues not resolved in early childhood spring into new life in "the second individuation process in adolescence" (Blos, 1967). At this stage, said Freud, "One of the most significant but also one of the most painful psychical achievements of the pubertal period is completed: detachment from parental authority" (1905b, p. 227). For the girl, says Peter Blos, "the prolonged and painful severance from the mother constitutes the major task of this period." Marshalling data from Helene Deutsch and Therese Benedek, he refers to "the strong regressive pull to the preoedipal mother and the panic which this surrender invokes" (1962, pp. 67–68). On the side of the girl's reality, Melanie Klein examined the mother's role: "If the mother has strong maternal feelings, she can remain unshaken in her love, can be patient and understanding, give help and advice when this is necessary, and yet allow the children to work out problems for themselves—and she may be able to do all this without asking much for herself. This is only possible, however, if her capacity for love has developed in such a way that she can make a strong identification both with her child, and with a wise mother of her own whom she keeps in mind" (1937, p. 319). Freud had said more pessimistically, "I learned that the duration of this attachment to the mother had been greatly underestimated . . . Indeed, one had to give due weight to the possibility that many a woman may remain arrested at the original mother-attachment and never properly achieve the change-over to men" (1931, p. 195). Discussing a group of homosexual female patients, Elaine Siegel finds: "They never doubted that they were female. But they were unable to traverse the usual developmental states that make a female into a sexually mature woman. For them, this calamity had to do with their inability to take full possession of their vaginas. Their narcissism remained coagulated. Their basic endowment for self-love and self-esteem never blossomed . . . They were expected to fulfill their mother's needs, not their own. From the very beginning, they received in one way or another the message that it was unacceptable, even dangerous, to become like their mothers" (1988, p. 22).

Two of the defenses available to the adolescent are secrecy and negativism. "Puberty," said Selma Fraiberg, "is the age of secrecy. It closes the door upon the prying adult . . . It hoards its secrets" (1955, p. 264). In our two fairy tales, the heroines hoped they would be able to keep their explorations secret from the mother-figures—to no avail. Her secret discovered, the girl resorts to negativism and denies she opened the door or entered the room, even denies knowing how her hair (or finger) became gold. Freud saw prohibition of masturbation as a motive for rebellion against the mother or mother-substitute (1931, p. 232). Anna Freud saw adolescent negativism as a defense against regression to "primary identification with the love object," feared by the individual as "a threat to the intactness of the ego" (1952, p. 259). The heroine refuses to answer the mother's questions about the forbidden room. The mother will not tolerate this insubordination. Looking at possible motives in the mother, Helene Deutsch theorized, "The mother feels abandoned, and as a result of her fear of losing her daughter, together with her fear of the consequences of her daughter's independence, she intensifies her wooing or attempts to exert an authoritarian power over her" (1945, p. 307). Karen Horney referred to a more hostile maternal motive: the "secret aim of thwarting the daughter in her female development" (1967, p. 179).

The heroine is now magically struck dumb and banished to a wilderness. What can this mean? Speech develops during the anal phase, which is also the phase of struggles over autonomy, with obstinacy as a cardinal feature (Freud, 1908a). Fenichel referred to the ability to speak as "a sign of potency" (1945, p. 300). Says Ellen Handler Spitz, "voice is . . . an affirmer of self, a confirmer of identity and self-sufficiency" (1987, p. 535); also, "To find one's own voice is to be able also to choose silence. It is to be able to make a ring of inclusion and a ring of exclusion, and thus to become independent—of the voice of the mother" (p. 538). The heroine has excluded the mother and, talion-fashion, has had her voice, independence, and autonomy taken away. Physiologically, loss of speech is due to swelling or spasm of the vocal cords, which can occur as a conversion symptom in conflict over the wish to shout in anger, "Yes! I did it and I'm glad! I don't need you any more!" versus saying in fear, "I'm sorry, Mother! Don't hurt me, don't desert me!" (Carol Sullivan, 1989). It may involve libidinal or hostile oral wishes (Breuer and Freud, 1895, p. 25; Fenichel, 1945, pp. 224, 300, 313–314; Freud, 1905a). "Dumb" can also mean "stupid"—bringing to mind the old superstition that masturbation will make a person into a stupid idiot, a "dummy." In their article, "The Wish Not to Know," Robert Lane and Robert Storch, in an extensive review of the literature on pseudoretardation, explain that particular kind of being dumb as, among other things, a mode of hiding one's curiosity and/or sexual awareness to avoid parental wrath and the wish "to remain unknowing, stupid and dependent on an omnipotent symbiotic mother in order to retain her love" (1984, pp. 58–62).

Freud equated dumbness with concealment, which is indeed our heroine's wish in refusing to answer (1913c, p. 247). Moses Laufer (1976, p. 204) refers to the feeling of "*deadlock*" the adolescent reaches in the struggle against regressive wishes—and indeed, loss of voice seems an image of deadlock, and *is* a deadlock of the vocal cords. In "The Theme of the Three Caskets," Freud saw dumbness as a symbol for death itself, drawing evidence from *King Lear,* in which Cordelia is banished for keeping silent and ends by dying; and from two Grimm's tales, "The Twelve Brothers" and "The Six Swans." In all of these, the heroine *voluntarily* remains mute—in the last-named fairy tales, to save her brothers from a spell (her death for theirs) (1913c)—while the heroine in our two tales is *made* mute by a spell. The "spell" can be seen as a projection of the girl's resentment of her mother's interference, or as a symbolic castration (Fenichel, 1945, p. 224).

The isolation of the heroine in a forest takes place in too many fairy tales not to have some special meaning: not only in "Mother Hildegarde," "Our Lady's Child," "The Twelve Brothers," and "The Six Swans," but also in "Snow White" and "The Sleeping Beauty." Might this mean a sort of "time out" between puberty and marriage? It could symbolize the "inner emptiness, grief and sadness" felt when closeness to parents has been rejected or lost by the adolescent and has not yet been replaced by a new relationship (Peter Blos, 1962, p. 100). The theme of isolation at menarche and during menstruation in general was described by Freud (1917) and by Bettelheim (1962), who speculates this was either from fear of menstrual blood or from envy of the power inherent in it. Bettelheim quotes the following fascinating passage from G. Devereux: "While Italian peasants ascribe nefarious powers to menstruating women, they also believe that at the time of her monthly period she rises a notch in the social hierarchy; the peasant woman becomes a lady, the latter a noblewoman, the noblewoman a queen, while the queen becomes identified with the Madonna—in fact, menstruation specifically proclaims woman's kinship with the Madonna" (1962, p. 252n). Stronger connections emerge regarding the reverence and awe accorded virgin goddesses and mother goddesses—the power/taboo associated with their virginity and with their menstruation—and also the association of these goddesses as well as menstruating women with isolated spots in forest huts or sacred groves (Freud, 1913a, 1917; Graves, 1960, 1966; Hale, 1965; Hamilton, 1942; Payne, 1966). The virgin goddesses were attended by girls who sometimes began their service when quite young and were expected to remain loyal and as chaste as the goddess herself, for example, the famous Vestal Virgins of ancient Rome. These goddesses were sometimes depicted as vengeful, but also as protecting fertility, childbirth, and newborns, as were moon-goddesses (James, 1960).

"Since ancient times," says Bettelheim, "the near-impenetrable forest in which we get lost has symbolized the dark, hidden, near-impenetrable world of our unconscious" (1977, p. 94). The period of isolation in our stories could thus be a metaphor for a difficult but perhaps fruitful waiting for a confused and thorny adolescent unconscious to disentangle itself.

What of the tree itself, the tree in which the princess in "Mother Hildegarde," the maidens in "The Twelve Brothers" and "The Six Swans," and the girl in "Our Lady's Child" were dwelling when the prince found them? An early Sumerian goddess, Belili, was a goddess of trees "as well as a Moon-goddess, Love-goddess and Underworld-goddess . . . Originally every tree was hers, and the Goidelic *Bile,* 'sacred tree,' the medieval Latin *billa* and *billus,* 'branch, trunk of tree,' and the English *billet* are recollections of her name" (Graves, 1966, p. 58). Freud discussed the resemblance of the Portuguese word for wood, *madeira,* to Latin, Spanish and Italian words for mother (*mater, madre*) (1916–1917, p. 160). Jung referred to "the cult of the Great Mother and her symbol, the tree" (1964, p. 81). The resemblance of our heroine to an ancient sylvan goddess is increasing.

Whereas a tree might be seen as a phallic symbol, in our tales it does not seem to be—unless the tree of the virgin goddess is a symbol of a hidden female phallus, which enables the heroine to withhold her assertiveness and bide her time until the king comes riding. Rapunzel's tower, up which Dame Gothel climbs, is a symbol of her own body, possessed by her mother; perhaps also a fantasy phallus desirable to the enchantress—but why, then, would the prince climb it? No, the tree in these tales is a woman-tree—perhaps a mother-surrogate, a refuge until the time is ripe for rescue.

And now the long golden hair she weaves about herself in place of clothes. One thinks of Lady Godiva; tales similar to hers have been found all over Europe. The man who peeped at her went blind; her radiant beauty *must* have been that of a goddess! And golden was the crowning glory of "the Love and Death goddess, Freye, alias Frigg, Hold, Held, Hilde, Goda, or Ostara," says Graves (1966, p. 403), adding, "Hilde was at home in the Milky Way" (Hilde=Hildegarde?).

Mary Magdalene, too, had long golden hair and, according to apocryphal traditions, went through a period of isolation in the wilderness, during which her clothes fell away and she had only her long hair for covering. Leach (1988) describes a Donatello figure of her thus, in the Baptistry at Florence. He also describes and furnishes reproductions of a similar portrayal painted in a triptych in 1518 by the Flemish Master of the Legend of Saint Mary Magdalene. In Assisi's Basilica of Saint Francis, a side chapel by Giotto (c.1300) portrays her legend in frescoes, including the scene where she is clothed only in her hair. A beautiful woodcarving of Magdalene by Tilman Riemenschneider (c.1500), in the Bavarian National Museum in Munich, presents her with her long hair clinging to but covering her naked body and limbs. In all these images of the naked woman clothed in her hair, there must be a common theme.

Long hair bespeaks power, as in Rapunzel, and as in another Grimm's tale about "The Goose Girl," who protects her hair from a thieving shepherd boy who hopes to gain some special power by pulling out some strands for himself (Bettelheim, 1977, p. 142). The long golden hair of the goddesses enumerated by Graves surely symbolized their power. Since tradition has it that Magdalene was a former prostitute, her long golden or red-gold hair, as depicted by artists over the centuries, is a symbol of her power to attract men sexually. What adolescent girl has not had fantasies of awesome attractiveness—goddess fantasies, princess fantasies, femme fatale or prostitute fantasies—fed by the new sense of her own sexuality, a sense that her newly developed body and her crown of hair may exert such a potent spell that a man will be drawn to her from miles away, without her even saying a word. Our heroine's power, however, is only latent, for she cannot assert herself.

The next section of the tales can be seen as the rescue fantasy of the pubertal girl: "Mother, if you don't love me any more, *some one* will." A passive fantasy it is, as the young king carries her unprotesting into marriage. Is this passivity a reaction on the part of an adolescent girl to her own internal developmental conflicts, or is there a contribution to it from reality? Freud claimed that the mother of the newly married girl "is unwilling to give up the possession of her daughter; she distrusts the stranger to whom her daughter has been delivered, and shows a tendency to maintain the dominating position to which she became accustomed at home" (1913a, p. 21). He might have added: if the daughter has not been able to relinquish the preoedipal or negative oedipal bond.

And now comes the uncanny part of the story. Instead of "and so they were married and lived happily ever after," we find the young queen, still refusing to confess, losing three babies to the unrelenting mother, and letting it appear that she has cannibalized her own children (this also occurs in "The Six Swans"). In Freud's "Three Essays on Sexuality" (1905b), he described "the oral or . . . cannibalistic pregenital sexual organization" whose aim is "the incorporation of the object," the prototype of later identification processes. Later, he wrote, "The ego wants to incorporate this object into itself, and, in accordance with the oral or cannibalistic phase of libidinal development in which it is, it wants to do so by devouring it" (1917, pp. 249–250). Esther Menaker writes, "The child incorporates the strict mother image as part of his own ego which demands punishment out of guilt for his sadistic impulses. This internalization and the taking of the guilt upon oneself perpetuates the relationship to the mother and stands in the way of separation from her" (1982, p. 53). Melanie Klein claimed that when the mother frustrates the infant by weaning it from the breast, "the child himself desires to destroy the libidinal object by biting, devouring and cutting" (1928, p. 187). The wish soon becomes more specifically a wish to destroy the mother's womb and the children in it—then "the girl anticipates retribution in the form of destruction of her own capacity for motherhood . . . and of her own children" (1928, p. 194). This Klein saw as the equivalent in girls of the castration anxiety experienced by boys (1932, p. 31).

From the side of reality, there is the mother's unconscious to consider. Robert Lane and Saralea Chazan observe: "Some women, upon giving birth, are surprised by a newly felt sympathy for this cannibalistic witch. Though they would rarely express their feeling consciously, they may feel a desire to lick and nibble their newborn children. How often have we heard an adult say to a young child, 'You are so delicious I am going to eat you up'" (1989, p. 329). These authors condense and summarize material on the ubiquity of the witch as a fear-fantasy. Helene Deutsch referred to fear of cannibalism as one of the *rationalizations* for the taboo of menstruating women (1944, p. 153).

At this point in our two fairy tales, there seems to be some confusion as to who is the witch, who the victim. The young queen could be projecting her own archaic oral wishes, in somewhat prettied-up form (stealing instead of eating), onto the powerful mother and expecting talion punishment. She could be feeling guilty over envious wishes to take over adult privileges. She could be assessing correctly her mother's disapproval of finding pleasure in her own body, or her mother's demand for perfect obedience, or her mother's need to possess the daughter's body in symbiotic union. Or she could be projecting her own wish to remain a dependent, cared-for little girl who stays on as mother's helper forever. At any rate, she loses her right to be a mother for stubbornly refusing to reveal her secret to the Mother who can move heaven and earth.

Defensive denial fails and splitting of the mother-figure returns: The earlier hostile stepmother who tried to kill her is reincarnated as the king's mother, who wants the young queen destroyed—a paranoid fantasy. Having accepted passively the punishment meted out by her protectress, she is unable to own the hostile reaction she must have felt, consciously or unconsciously, and must project it—this time onto her mother-in-law, who now appears as dangerously hostile. Further, if she can take the attitude of innocent victim—"I never tried to take the king from his mother; I never competed; *she's* the competitive one, not me"—she is defending herself from the emergence of oedipal wishes. One must also, however, look at the reality that many a mother of sons does indeed bear ill-will toward her daughters-in-law. In either case, just as the girl's father was a cipher who failed to protect his daughter from her stepmother, so the young king proves to be a cipher as well, letting his mother and the townspeople determine the fate of his wife. Why are the men in these two tales so ineffectual, so different from the active princes in better-known tales? The answer seems to be because the heroine is still ambivalently attached to her mother. The discomfort in this theme may also be the reason these tales are not among the continually popular ones. Says Silverman in a recent article on female bonding, "The girl's intense envy and destructive fantasies intensify her restitutive needs and thus cement tightly her connectedness with her mother" (1987, p. 209). And, write Lane and Chazan, "it is the conflict in relationship to the primary object which must be resolved before true heterosexual feelings can be established" (1988, p. 8).

And so the tales march toward their final crisis: lacking the power of speech by which she could defend herself, the heroine is pronounced a witch and condemned to be burned at the stake. The symbolism is brutally phallic, but also oral: Freud wrote, "The warmth that is radiated by fire calls up the same sensation that accompanies a state of sexual excitation, and the shape and movements of a flame suggest a phallus in activity . . . When we speak of the 'devouring fire' of love and of 'licking' flames—thus comparing the flame to a tongue—we have not moved so very far from the mode of thinking of our primitive ancestors" (1932, p. 190). For her oral desires (need to consume mother) and her oral withholding (defense against fear of being consumed by mother), she is to be consumed, annihilated, by a heat that is too intense. Fire could also represent rage, unconscious burning rage at the mother figure turned against herself, denying herself the joys of marriage, children, even life rather than cede a point to mother.

By 1931, Freud was agreeing with Melanie Klein: "We find the little girl's oral and sadistic wishes, in a form forced on them by early repression, as a fear of being killed by her mother" (p. 237). On the side of reality, he adds, "It is impossible to say how often this fear of the mother is supported by an unconscious hostility on the mother's part which is sensed by the girl" (1931, p. 237). Melanie Klein began to modify her views in the direction of some input from the environment, writing that children's destructive fantasies and fears, though occurring "even in the most favorable circumstances, are necessarily very much increased by unfavorable conditions and unpleasant experiences" (1945, pp. 338–339). Harry Stack Sullivan claimed, "The tension of anxiety, when present in the mothering one, induces anxiety in the infant" (1953, p. 41), and since anxiety interferes with the mother's cooperation in relieving needs and her cooperation "is necessary to keep the infant alive," this maladaptation can feel like, and can indeed *be*, a threat to life itself (pp. 53–54). From this grows a "structure of anxiety" which may reappear in adolescence (p. 9). David Winnicott claimed that "growing up means taking the parent's place. *It really does*. . . . In the total unconscious fantasy belonging to growth at puberty and in adolescence, there is *the death of someone*" (1971, p. 145) and hence the unconscious wish to kill the parent leads by projection to the fantasy of the self being put to death instead. Dorothy Bloch finds fear of being killed by a parent to be a universal among children; she also finds the intensity of this fear "depends on the incidence of traumatic events and on the degree of violence and of love they have experienced" (1978, p. 3); further, that the child's "need for defenses was compounded by his inevitably violent responses to his parents' violence or violent wishes and feelings" (p. 6). Bloch credits Hyman Spotnitz with having pointed out that Freud omitted an important section from the Oedipus legend in explicating his theory: When

Oedipus was born, it was prophesied that he would grow up to kill his father and marry his mother, so his parents tried to have him killed in infancy to abort the dread prophecy.*

To return to the stories: In the midst of the flames, the heroine's "heart melted away within her" (Pyle, 1887, p. 201), "the hard ice of pride melted, her heart was moved by repentance" (Grimm, 1944, p. 28) and she confessed that she did indeed go into the forbidden room, see what she shouldn't see, touch what she shouldn't touch. "Then Mother Hildegarde smiled till her face shone as white as the moon" (Pyle, 1887, p. 201) and total forgiveness was bestowed. Rain falls (a tearful reunion), putting out the flames; the three children are returned, and there is joy in the castle. Yet is there truly a case for joy? Moses Laufer saw, after a feeling of deadlock in the adolescents' struggle for autonomy, an ominous next step: "a feeling of *giving in,* which is then followed by a feeling of *surrender* . . . as if they have accepted that genitality, with regard to both object relationships and gratification, either cannot or must not be attained" (1976, p. 304). The uncanny aura of our two fairy tales hovered about the theft of the babies, the smearing of the lips with blood, the requirement to confess or die, and the implications of surrender: pride melted, heart melted—what was left of the heroine's self?

According to Freud, "an uncanny experience occurs either when infantile complexes which have been repressed are once more revived by some impression, or when primitive beliefs which have been surmounted seem once more to be confirmed." In fairy tales, he said, you don't get that uncanny feeling because "the world of reality is left behind from the very start" (1919, pp. 249–250). But these two tales glide perilously close to the shores of a dark and frightening reality: the possibility of engulfment by the archaic mother, the loss of a life of adult meaning. And no brother or other hero came riding to rescue the heroine from death, as in Bluebeard (who was about to kill her for exploring the forbidden room)—only Mother herself. Was it the young queen's autonomy, her individuality, that melted in a merging with mother?

Or can we look at it another way? Can the heroine's uncommunicativeness toward her mother be seen as a self-defeating negativism,

* It is hard to deal with the fact that many parents wish, consciously or unconsciously, to kill their children and that so many of them do actually abuse them. Public repression and denial kept these realities out of the media until the mid-1970s, and the laws that were eventually passed are still poorly enforced, the unfortunate truths still incompletely realized.

which fixated her in unrealistic childishness? Mother Hildegarde/Our Lady did not, after all, punish the heroine for *visiting* the forbidden room, but for refusing to admit it. In this light, the uncanny section can be viewed as metaphor for a young woman's unresolved infantile hostility toward her mother erupting in cannibalistic fantasies toward her own babies and spoiling the pleasure of motherhood for her. It is possible then to see the "melting" metaphor as a melting of defenses which are blocking a resolution of her distorted view of her mother, or as a step toward loving reparation. On this level, her eventual confession can be seen not as loss of autonomy but rather as a mature willingness to take responsibility for her own deeds.

The theme of the two fairy tales examined here is the nexus of conflicts every girl must encounter in differentiating herself from her mother. The conflicts are many faceted: internally spurred, externally aggravated, but basically preoedipal. Her tasks involve overcoming dependence on her mother's physical presence; asserting her need to grow, explore, and separate; getting past her fear of her mother's disapproval; developing the courage to take responsibility for her actions. None of these tasks can be completed without the integration of her genitals into her body image. The "forbidden room" is the essence of her femaleness, that which permits her to be her own woman, a young goddess. Only by taking proud possession of her "forbidden room" can she hope to realize her productive potential.

References

Abraham, K. (1911). Observations of the cult of the mother and its symbols in individual and folk psychology. In *Clinical papers and essays on psychoanalysis.* New York: Brunner/Mazel, 1955.

Bernstein, I. (1975). Integrative aspects of masturbation. In I. M. Marcus & J. J. Francis (Eds.), *Masturbation from infancy to senescence.* New York: International Universities Press.

Bettelheim, B. (1962). *Symbolic wounds.* New York: Collier.

Bettelheim, B. (1977). *The uses of enchantment.* New York: Vintage.

Bloch, D. (1978). *So the witch won't eat me.* Boston: Houghton-Mifflin.

Blos, P. (1962). *On adolescence.* New York: Free Press.

Blos, P. (1967). The second individuation process of adolescence. *Psychoanalytic Study of the Child, 22,* 162–186.

Breuer, J., & Freud, S. (1895). Studies in Hysteria. *Standard Edition, 2.*

Deutsch, H. (1932). Homosexuality in women. *International Journal of Psychoanalysis, 14,* 34–56.

Deutsch, H. (1944). *Psychology of women: Girlhood.* New York: Grune & Stratton.

Deutsch, H. (1945). *Psychology of women: Motherhood.* New York: Grune & Stratton.

Eidelberg, L. (1945). A contribution to the study of the masturbation fantasy. *International Journal of Psychoanalysis, 26,* 127–137.

Fenichel, O. (1945). *The psychoanalytic theory of neurosis.* New York: W. W. Norton.

Fraiberg, S. (1954). Tales of the discovery of the secret treasure. *Psychoanalytic Study of the Child, 9,* 218–241.

Fraiberg, S. (1955). Some considerations in the introduction to therapy in puberty. *Psychoanalytic Study of the Child, 10,* 264–288.

Freud, A. (1952). Studies in passivity. *The writings of Anna Freud.* New York: International Universities Press, 1968.

Freud, S. (1895). Studies in Hysteria. *Standard Edition, 2.*

Freud, S. (1900). The interpretation of dreams. *Standard Edition, 5,* 339–630.

Freud, S. (1901). On dreams. *Standard Edition, 5,* 631ff.

Freud, S. (1905a). Fragment of an analysis of a case of hysteria. *Standard Edition, 7,* 7–122.

Freud, S. (1905b). Three essays on sexuality. *Standard Edition, 7,* 125–243.

Freud, S. (1908a). Character and anal erotism. *Standard Edition, 9,* 167–176.

Freud, S. (1908b). Family romances. *Standard Edition, 9,* 235–244.

Freud, S. (1911a). Dreams in folklore. *Standard Edition, 12,* 180–204.

Freud, S. (1911b). Great is Diana of the Ephesians. *Standard Edition, 12,* 342–344.

Freud, S. (1913a). Totem and taboo. *Standard Edition, 13,* 1–164.

Freud, S. (1913b). The occurrence in dreams of material from fairy tales. *Standard Edition, 12,* 279–288.

Freud, S. (1913c). The theme of the three caskets. *Standard Edition, 12,* 289–302.

Freud, S. (1915). A case of paranoia running counter to the psychoanalytic theory of the disease. *Standard Edition, 14,* 261–272.

Freud, S. (1916–1917). Introductory lectures on psychoanalysis. *Standard Edition, 15.*

Freud, S. (1917). Mourning and melancholia. *Standard Edition, 14,* 243–258.

Freud, S. (1918). The taboo of virginity. *Standard Edition, 11,* 191–208.

Freud, S. (1919). The uncanny. *Standard Edition, 17,* 217–252.

Freud, S. (1920). The psychogenesis of a case of homosexuality in a woman. *Standard Edition, 18,* 145–174.

Freud, S. (1931). Female sexuality. *Standard Edition, 21,* 225–246.

Freud, S. (1932). The acquisition and control of fire. *Standard Edition, 22,* 187–196.

Freud, S. (1933). New introductory lectures on psychoanalysis. *Standard Edition, 22,* 5–184.

Graves, R. (1960). *The Greek myths.* New York: Penguin.

Graves, R. (1966). *The white goddess* (rev. ed.). New York: Farrar Strauss & Giroux.

Grimm, J., & Grimm, W. K. (1944). *The complete Grimm's fairy tales.* New York: Pantheon.

Hale, W. H. (1965). *The Horizon book of Ancient Greece.* New York: American Heritage.

Hamilton, E. (1942). *Mythology.* Boston: Little, Brown.

Horney, K. (1967). *Feminine psychology.* New York: W. W. Norton.

James, E. O. (1960). *The ancient gods.* New York: Putnam.

Jung, C. (1964). Approaching the unconscious. In C. Jung, M. L. von Franz, J. L. Henderson, J. Jacobi, & A. Jaffe (Eds.), *Man and his symbols.* New York: Doubleday.
Klein, M. (1928). Early stages of the Oedipus conflict. In *Love, guilt, and reparation, 1921–1945.* New York: Delacorte Press, 1975.
Klein, M. (1932). *The psychoanalysis of children.* New York: Delacorte Press, 1975.
Klein, M. (1945). The Oedipus complex in the light of early anxieties. In *Love, guilt and reparation, 1921–1945.* New York: Delacorte Press, 1975.
Lane, R. C., & Storch, R. (1984). The wish not to know. *Current Issues in Psychoanalytic Practice, 1,* 53–72.
Lane, R. C., & Chazan, S. E. (1988). Psychoanalytic perspectives on the treatment of early adolescent girls. *Journal of Contemporary Psychotherapy, 18,* 5–15.
Lane, R. C., & Chazan, S. E. (1989). Symbols of terror: The witch/vampire, the spider and the shark. *Psychoanalytic Psychology, 6,* 325–342.
Laufer, M. (1976). The central masturbation fantasy. *Psychoanalytic Study of the Child, 31,* 297–316.
Leach, E. (1988). Late medieval representations of St. Mary Magdalene. *Psychoanalytic Review, 75,* 95–109.
Mahler, M. (1968). *On human symbiosis and the vicissitudes of individuation.* New York: International Universities Press.
Mahler, M., Pine, F., & Bergman, A. (1975). *The psychological birth of the human infant.* New York: Basic Books.
Menaker, E. (1982). *Otto Rank: A rediscovered legend.* New York: Columbia University Press.
Payne, R. (1966). *The Horizon book of Ancient Rome.* New York: American Heritage.
Pyle, H. (1887). *The wonder clock.* New York: Harper & Bros.
Rank, O. (1914). *The myth of the birth of the hero.* New York: Vintage Press, 1964.
Sexton, A. (1971). *Transformations.* Boston: Houghton-Mifflin.
Sharpe, E. F. (1937). *Dream analysis.* London: Hogarth Press.
Siegel, E. V. (1988). *Female homosexuality: Choice without volition.* Hillsdale, NJ: Analytic Press.
Silverman, D. K. (1987). Female bonding. *Psychoanalytic Review, 74,* 201–216.
Spitz, E. H. (1987). Separation-individuation in a cycle of songs. *Psychoanalytic Study of the Child, 42,* 531–543.
Steel, F. A. (1918). *English fairy tales.* New York: Macmillan.
Sullivan, C. (1989). Presentation on voice disorders before the psychoanalytic practitioners of Long Island, December 3.
Sullivan, H. S. (1953). *The interpersonal theory of psychiatry.* New York: W. W. Norton.
von Franz, M.-L. (1964). The process of individuation. In M.-L. von Franz, C. Jung, J. L. Henderson, J. Jacobi, & A. Jaffe (Eds.), *Man and his symbols.* New York: Doubleday.
Weimer, S. (1978). Using fairy tales in psychotherapy: Rapunzel. *Bulletin of the Menninger Clinic, 42,* 25–34.
Wickes, F. G. (1927). *The inner world of childhood.* New York: Appleton-Century.
Winnicott, D. W. (1971). *Playing and reality.* London: Tavistock Press.